POLICE, PRISONS, POLITICS, & POWER I

POLICE, PRISONS, POLITICS, & POWER I

HOWARD SAFFOLD

Police, Prisons, Politics, & Power I

Copyright © 2024 by Howard Saffold. All rights reserved.

No part of this publication may be reproduced, stored in a retrieval system or transmitted in any way by any means, electronic, mechanical, photocopy, recording or otherwise without the prior permission of the author except as provided by USA copyright law.

The opinions expressed by the author are not necessarily those of URLink Print and Media.

1603 Capitol Ave., Suite 310 Cheyenne, Wyoming USA 82001
1-888-980-6523 | admin@urlinkpublishing.com

URLink Print and Media is committed to excellence in the publishing industry.

Book design copyright © 2024 by URLink Print and Media. All rights reserved.

Published in the United States of America
ISBN 978-1-68486-669-4 (Paperback)
ISBN 978-1-68486-671-7 (Digital)
06.05.24

DEDICATION

To my wonderful wife, Carol Saffold,
thank you for your patience and understanding and love
and for being the best wife a man could ever have.
Thank you for standing by me and believing in me.
I love you and miss you every single day.
To my beloved parents Dewitt and Eva Saffold
My one and only paternal aunt,
dear beloved Ruth Ann Saffold-Davis
and to my beloved mother and father-in-law,
Ralph and Ernestine Randall

TABLE OF CONTENTS

FOREWORD ix
NOTES FROM THE PUBLISHER xi
PREFACE xiii
INTRODUCTION xv
Chapter 1:   CHILDHOOD MEMORIES 1
Chapter 2:   HIGH SCHOOL DAYS 10
Chapter 3:   MILITARY SERVICE & MARRIAGE 23
Chapter 4:   BECOMING A COP 28
Chapter 5:   A SECOND RUDE AWAKENING 31
Chapter 6:   FORMING THE AAPL 53
Chapter 7:   BREAKING THE CODE 58
Chapter 8:   AAPL MEMBERSHIP TAKES A TOLL 64
Chapter 9:   BLOWING THE WHISTLE 87
Chapter 10: THE DISCRIMINATION LAWSUIT 95
Chapter 11: NATIONAL BLACK POLICE ASSOCIATION 102
Chapter 12: THE HAROLD WASHINGTON ERA 106
Chapter 13: POSITIVE ANTI-CRIME THRUST 127
REFERENCES 139
AFRO-AMERICAN PATROLMAN'S LEAGUE ROSTER 143

FOREWORD

Police, Prisons, Politics & Power is the perfect topic for Howard Saffold to reflect upon as he reviews his life and career. Howard has dedicated most of his life to service both within the Chicago Police Department and service within the community, especially the Black community and communities of color. His main contribution with the Department and the community was to hold the Department accountable for discriminatory practices within the rank and file as well as among officers within the community. This story relates how he developed programs to decrease violence and provide programs for youth and young adults – programs that moved them toward becoming responsible citizens and making a positive contribution to the wider community.

Saffold has a deep compassion for those in prison and has challenged people of faith to provide prison ministries that not only offer spiritual support but seek justice within the justice system. The book tells how he is never satisfied with mediocrity and continues to struggle with ways the community could empower and liberate its people.

Howard's life story helps the reader to see how he grew to be a leader, making genuine contributions to the society. His story of survival, courage and strength should be celebrated and honored. He is an unsung hero and the world is better because Howard served.

Rev. Sharon Ellis Davis, PhD, M.Div., Retired Police Officer, Pastor & Seminary Professor

NOTES FROM THE PUBLISHER

"I am the Law!"

This is the assumption made by many law enforcement officers and many ordinary citizens. This belief has been the basis for many actions taken by officers of the law. Unfortunately, due to the pervasive racial bias that exists in the United States of America, the combination of these two elements has resulted in decades of unlawful acts, bodily harm, and death for Black citizens at the hands of white police officers.

This book, written by Howard Saffold, tells the story of the journey of a Black man, born and raised in Chicago, who became a police officer who never forgot his racial heritage and commitment to enforcing the law. His duty was to maintain the peace, protect the people and businesses. When he discovered a person or persons violating the law, it was his responsibility to bring those individuals to the court in order to allow the judge and jury to decide upon their innocence or guilt. This is because in the criminal justice system in our country, the person arrested is presumed innocent until proven guilty.

The author describes his experiences as a patrolman, working with white partners and in various communities. His concerns about improper handling of minority offenders led him to join with Edward "Buzz" Palmer, Curtis Cowsen, Nate Silas, Wille Ware, Jack DeBonnet, Renault Robinson and Frank Lee to form the Afro-American Patrolmen's League (AAPL) in 1968. The mission of AAPL was to reduce the unlawful racist acts by white police officers and to enhance the role of Black patrolmen in the Chicago Police Department (CPD). This has made the AAPL and its leadership the target of retaliation by the powerful leadership in the CPD and the political establishment.

The recent incidents in various parts of the nation provide clear evidence of the need for organizations that advocate for justice and fairness for Black citizens. Howard Saffold has made it clear that there is a need for better training and periodic psychological evaluation of police officers. The author has continued on his journey to improve the criminal justice system with his formation of Positive Anti-Crime Thrust (PACT). This book will give the reader a better understanding of the problems in law enforcement. It will give some insight into what work has been done and is being done to make the criminal justice system fairer.

PREFACE

As I contemplated the question "how and why is this book about police community relations in America relevant today?" I couldn't help but also ask who the heck cares? After reflecting on my experience in the criminal justice arena for the past 50 years those questions took me to a place I'm calling the *reality lane*, and that *reality lane* is where my answers came from.

The stakeholders need to care. That broad category of people who are directly or indirectly impacted by actions or inactions on their part pertaining to this matter shook my 80-year old soul. If the society we are living in has any possibility of sustaining itself, we should all care.

Speaking from a spiritual perspective, this seems like a perfect time for each of us to do a little soul-searching in order to move into the reality lane. I tell a few stories in this book, hoping to raise a few personal questions of you. Is there anything you can do to help make this a better world? Is there anything you can stop doing that might help?

If nothing else, I hope the book will ignite a small spark of encouragement in you to give some thought to these questions. In other words, I hope reading the book will give *us* — and I put emphasis on *us* — something to think about; after all *we* — and I put emphasis on *we* — are in this place together.

This book lays the foundation for the work to be done. Let's do it!

INTRODUCTION

On April 4, 1968, Dr. Martin Luther King, Jr., one of our foremost leaders of the nonviolent Civil Rights Action Movement, was assassinated on a balcony in Memphis, Tennessee. His assassination triggered the outpouring of Black people's grief, pain, and anger in a series of riots in nearly 100 major American cities, including, Chicago, Baltimore, Louisville, Washington, D.C., and New York City, to name a few.

Just three short years prior, on February 21, 1965, Malcolm X, another prominent leader of the Human Rights movement, was murdered. The history of the nonstop struggle for justice of Black people in America is undeniable and long overdue for reconciliation. I note these two men in particular for two reasons. Number one, their names have continued to be mentioned in the world news arenas from the time of their original introductions, and two, both their lives ended in the time frame of my story. The legacies of both of these giants live on, along with countless other men, women and children, who have lost their lives in this seemingly endless effort to destroy a race of people who were brought upon this earth by the same God that most humans claim to be their creator. Consideration of all religions are respected by this writer. I personally believe many of us can bear witness to the fact that we are seeing evidence of a great number of sick, diabolical mindsets, who have been historically exhibiting enormous influential power overall. This element has surfaced shamelessly inside or at the head of some of the most prominent educational, political, financial and historical institutons in today's world. It's up to the decent, God-fearing people who want to live in a better world to both design and develop effective ways and means to make the dream of justice and equity a reality. A key challenge is to continue discussing this very difficult subject with people with whom you have to interact on a regular basis. I suspect that many Black and other non-white families, young and old, mostly young, have lost or are losing faith in too many of these institutions. I, as an elder, firmly believe that our younger generations deserve some tangible assurances from these institutions that their youthful hopes and dreams are worth retaining. The subject of this book is just a microcosm of our larger society.

My story begins with early childhood reflections (1950's), and segues through the late 50's and early 60's. By then I have discovered a way to engage life in a very meaningful way; to serve my community by connecting with and dedicating myself to a group of Black Chicago Policemen who had merged their energies together to form the Afro American Patrolmen's League, which was later named the Afro American Police League. As a relatively new member of the Chicago Police Department at that time, witnessing the racism from the inside inspired and motivated me to join with some fellow Black policemen in the formation of that organization.

This is my story. Won't you please come along with me in this effort to help, with the use of plain talk, determine how we as everyday people might change our approach to uniting our thoughts and energy for the purpos.e of exploring ways to make a better world for it's individuals, families and communities.

CHAPTER 1

CHILDHOOD MEMORIES

My parents, Dewitt Saffold and Eva Saffold, met as teenagers in Mississippi and came to Chicago from Mississippi in 1935. They were good parents, who married young, had a lot of children and too few resources. They left the south to make a better life for themselves and their children. It didn't go according to their plan, but they did the best they could with what they had. Their children never brought shame nor regret to them during their lifetime, and we were all proud of that truth. At the time of this writing, my parents, three brothers and one sister are deceased.

I was the middle child. I had two brothers and a sister, who were older, and two younger brothers and a younger sister. My older brother, Joe Louis, was the only one of us born in Lexington, Mississippi. The rest of us were all born right here in Chicago at the Cook County Hospital. When my parents separated in 1954, I went with my father because he had a firmer hand on the older four. By the time we moved, my oldest brother had married and moved out on his own. My three younger siblings stayed with my mother though grade school. We all eventually ended up in my father's house.

I remember one very cold Chicago winter morning when just my father and I were riding in his old out dated car. As we approached the mouth of the alley, a patch of ice under the light coat of snow caused the car to slide forward. A white man had just stepped into our path from the curb. The car was barely moving but had not completely stopped. We slid into the man who held onto the bumper to keep from sliding underneath the car. As the person pulled himself to his feet, I heard my father say in a low-pitched voice "Oh my God." This man looked to be about my father's age, mid-thirties. His face had turned blood red. "What the hell is wrong with you dammit, you SOB. Can't you drive?" I thought my father was going to ask him who he thought he was talking to. Never before had I seen a confrontation like that between a white man and a Black man. It was usually white and Black kids my age getting chesty with each other and fighting, if it came to that. So, I'm thinking my father is about to get it on. Instead, he was apologetic. I was about 9 or 10 years old, and I felt crushed. After several seconds of having his say, the guy walked away. My father let him get a few feet away before he rolled his window back up and we continued on our way. I must have looked very puzzled to my Dad. I sure felt strange and disappointed. He asked me if I had understood what had just happened. I said something like, "you almost got in a fight." He said, "You are right. But that would not have been a smart thing for me to do." He then went on to teach me a lesson that has remained with me from that day to this one. "First of all, I was at fault." He said, "You have to know when you are in the wrong. I am very glad that I had not really hurt the man. I would have a combination of problems right now. Without serious injury, that guy would still have had a right to sue me, and I would most likely have lost my insurance. He might have tried to sue me by claiming he was hurt. I'm glad he didn't try to do that." My dad went on to say, "I could have gotten angry about what he was saying and I could have said the same kind of junk back to him. We would not have been able to drive away as we did if he had gone to call the police. I would have gotten a ticket, been forced to go to court, and I probably would have paid some kind of fine that we can't afford." Finally, he said, "As long as he walked away and didn't try to hit you or me, I didn't care what he said."

For many years, I thought about that incident and my father's reaction. It took me awhile to understand what that attitude meant in the 1940's for a Black man in America. . I learned a lot about my old man and myself that day. Our closeness continued to grow as I matured. Over a decade later, I heard Malcolm X speak about how important it is to know when to try and save your head for a better day

When I reflect on my early education, I now realize that I was fortunate to have had a good beginning. I can remember when I was three or four years old, being excited about going to school because my older siblings were already in school. I was looking forward to it, and I could hardly wait. When I got to the George Maniere Elementary School, located at 1420 North Hudson Avenue, I focused mainly on my studies, trying to be a high achiever, and competing with the diverse ethnicities represented in the classroom. Our school and the surrounding community represented a microcosm of America. The immediate area had almost every ethnic group: Polish, Italian, Irish, Jewish, Latinos, Chinese, Japanese, and African American. In my first eight years, I was eager to learn, and I earned good grades. Our street, Clybourn Avenue, was a dividing line for schools. We often compared notes with our friends and cousins who lived on the opposite side of the street and thus, attended the predominately-Black school in the area. We could see a big difference in our textbooks compared to theirs.

We read things such as *Scholastic Magazine*, and we were actually learning about what was going on in the world beyond our community while in fourth and fifth grade. We were discussing civics, geography and budgets and these curricula were not taught in the predominately-Black schools. I recall a humorous cartoon in one of our take-home magazines that described an accident during a family's Thanksgiving dinner. The caption read, "The downfall of Turkey, the breaking up of China, and the overflowing of Greece." That cartoon was the subject of a classroom discussion about what was going on in those countries and throughout the world after World War II ended.

Classical music and futuristic scientific works in progress were also part of our studies. Some of the students (whose parents were our teachers) were visiting the Museum of Science and Industry as our class studied and discussed new developments. Even the levels of conversation for us as children were different. We were beginning to learn that while we enjoyed our fun filled events during summer vacation, going to Stanton Park, Seward Park, and the Lincoln Park Zoo, some of our classmates came back to school talking about trips they made to other cities in the U.S. as well as other countries around the world. As a young child, I began to realize that my world was limited in so many ways, and that my imagination and dreams were happening in other people's lives.

When part of our school burned down because of a fire, for a short time we had to take certain classes during the day at a Catholic School. I don't remember the name of that school, but I remember we had to learn a little bit about Catholicism and Catechism. We tried to explain this interruption to our cousins and friends on the other side of the street, but they really didn't know what we were talking about. The truth is, we didn't either, but the experience helped to broaden our horizons.

In those days, schools based their grading system on letters from E for Excellent to U for Unsatisfactory. I maintained all E's through eighth grade. I did not play around because my parents had us doing competitive kinds of things at home, like spelling bees, reading, and learning exercises. I could actually out-perform two of my older siblings. The only one of my siblings that was sharper than I was my brother, Joe. I could give my brother and sister who were right over me a little contest every now and then. I loved reading and spelling, and difficult words that I had to look up for the spelling and definition fascinated me.

The only down side of school was not having nice clothes or daily milk money. Not having the 3 or 4 cents for milk, every single day, was often embarrassing. We were from a family of seven children. To some of our more affluent surrounding neighbors, we were "those poor kids from over there on Clybourn Avenue."

Nevertheless, the quality of our early education was right there for everyone in the classroom to see.

Our education extended beyond the classroom. Living on the Near North Side of Chicago was an early learning experience. The City classified our neighborhood as an industrial strip. Right in front of my house, on the south side of the street, was a construction company, which at the time was called the Paschen Construction Company. Occasionally the large overhead garage door would open, and we would see one of the executives. We learned the name of Chris Paschen, who would emerge out onto Clybourn Avenue in a convertible Cadillac with two large boxer dogs sitting in the back of the car.

Behind my house was Sieben's Brewery. They had a huge beer hall. As I got older, some of us would go in and shine shoes near the front door facing Larrabee Street. To the north of my house on our side of the street was the Jefferson Ice Company, and to the south of my house, as you crossed Larrabee Street, was the White Way Sign Company, on Clybourn Avenue. There was a lot of industry in my community.

Down the middle of my street was the streetcar that we called "Big Red," because it was big and red. It came clanging and rattling down the street every day. All the sounds, smells, and sights were very distinct. You knew when the air hammer crew was working at Paschen. You could smell the brewery. You could see the White Way Sign Company's huge vertical lights forming a stream of flickering lights during the night. It was quite a scene back in those days.

People were driving in and out of the ice company buying ice all year long. A murder was committed in the factory part of the icehouse. There had been a robbery one night, and an employee was killed. Another crime scene evolved with one of the families in the neighborhood when two teenagers swiped a clump of Christmas trees from the truck dock. Footprints and thistles in the fresh snow led the manager and police straight to the basement coal shed, which was a few houses south of mine.

We talked about that all winter long. The factory eventually shut down, but the drive-up ice dispensary remained active.

I was introduced to jazz in the upstairs loft portion of the icehouse, which was converted into a community-focused incubator of sorts. The Slick Calvin group began to have Friday night jazz sets. They were not selling alcohol, so if a kid came in with some borrowed I.D. from the 18 and over crowd and brought no attention to himself, he could be exposed to local musicians who had it going on in those days.

To live in a poverty-stricken area that was replete with some necessities, the determination and creativity displayed was nothing short of being a magnificent blessing. Although there were many unaffordable features in the neighborhood, we also had plenty of affordable activities. We were in close proximity to the Chicago Park District's Stanton Park and Seward Park. We were close to the Isham YMCA (made famous by the late Johnny Weissmuller, the actor who played Tarzan). The Olivet Institute, a multi-level community center where the famous Harlem Globetrotters practiced on numerous occasions, was also available to us with after-school programs. We were in walking distance of the Oak Street Beach (Lake Front on the East boundaries of Chicago.). We were also near Riverview, one of the largest amusement parks in the area. We had three theaters in the area and every summer we looked forward to going to the annual Italian Fests and outdoor carnivals.

A regular scene in those days was the horse and buggy. Old man Charley had a stable and several ponies for rental. Some of the neighborhood fellows could earn money working with Charley during the spring, summer, and fall. If you could ride the pony to Lincoln Park, work the full day walking the pony with child riders and ride the pony back to the stable at the end of the day, you had a job. Most of the help would work one day and stay away for two. Charley worked every day, and he seemed to love what he was doing

Not every Black family on our block was quite as financially challenged as our household was. Roscoe Thomas, a World War

II veteran, and his wife Margie owned a mom-and-pop store that sold fresh meat and vegetables straight from South Water Market, aka Maxwell Street District, a local wholesale distribution center with remnants that still exist today. They were able to extend credit to families on the block. Our family had extended credit whenever we needed it. Some of those tight knit relationships have lasted for generations, until this very day. The storeowners were affectionately known to all of the children on the block as Uncle Roscoe and Aunt Margie.

Unfortunately, Roscoe and Margie experienced tragedy early in our teenaged years when their only daughter when a car accident claimed the life of their only daughter, Charlene, who was on her way home from college. The pain and sorrow brought the neighbors even closer to each other. Charlene had become a willing tutor to many of us who were a few years younger. Her five first cousins, the Thomas brothers, were like brothers to us all.

Now when it came to having recreation money, we of lesser wealth learned to be creative. We could make a scooter by using worn-out street roller skates and attaching them to a two by four plank made of wood and then attaching the plank with the metal wheels to a wooden milk crate. The tools were a claw hammer and a few spike nails. We could make a bow and arrow with cut-off tree limbs or bamboo poles and string. Our lumber came from Hines Lumber Co., which was in the 1500 block on North Clybourn Avenue, and we got scrap rubber bands, to make slingshots, from the nearby rubber factory.

Although we were considered by the neighbors to be pretty good kids, we did have a couple of encounters with the police. When I was about ten-years old, my friends and I were in a playground, which was near a filling station. As matter of fact, the father of one of the guys in our little group worked at that gas station as a mechanic. A banana vender had his truck parked there and was having some work done on it. He had a truckload of bananas and a gate pulled across the back of the truck to discourage vandals. Guys could make what we called a match shooter with stick matches, an empty thread spool, and a half-inch rubber band, and could then actually project a match by pulling the band back, similar to a miniature bow and arrow. The big boys had a stick match, shooting at the tailgate of the truck. All of a sudden, smoke started coming through the top of the truck, and then the next thing we knew, the truck was in full blaze. The police arrived and locked up all of us. They took us to the Hudson Avenue Station, contacted our parents, and tried to pin the crime on us. We were released to our parents and not held in jail.

My work experience began when I was still in grade school. I helped my father sell Fuller products because he was not able to climb all of those stairs to the homes of our customers. My Dad's lungs had practically collapsed from working in the steel mill in Melrose Park, Illinois.

When I graduated from Manierre Grammar School, it was a big deal for a little guy with great dreams. I did well in grammar school, and graduation was exciting. With my shoestring necktie, blue suede loafers, and my first new suit, I was too clean. I owned a nice hand me down, wool suit, purchased from the goodwill store, but I was graduating in the month of June. I was able to help buy the new gabardine suit with the money I made helping my dad sell Fuller products.

The second time I was arrested by the police was when a group of us teenagers were sitting on a railing in front of our friend's house. His mother was gone, and he couldn't come outside, but we could talk to him through the window. So, we were sitting out there in front of his house talking and some kind of way, the conversation got heated, and he ended up throwing a cup of water through the screen on one of the guys sitting on the railing. This guy went around there and kicked the boy's door in. It wasn't that secure on the hinges anyway. When his mother came home, she called the police. She didn't know our names, only our nicknames. That's when I learned that the police use nicknames and street names to catch people. They caught us and took us all to jail for breaking and entering. That particular day, a few of us had things in our pockets that we should not have had, like dice, playing cards, and other things that thirteen and fourteen-year-old boys carried back in those days. Once again, they released us. At that time, it was still the policy of the Youth Division to summon parents for incidents of that nature. Just like the earlier arrest, this one also didn't result in us being held in jail. No record was being created and as a result, when I later applied for work as a police officer, I had no record of any kind.

CHAPTER 2

HIGH SCHOOL DAYS

Just as my two older brothers had to start earning money as they entered high school, in my freshman year, I started with a job as a messenger downtown in the Loop, delivering for A-1 Secretarial Service. I used to carry cylinders of dictation tapes to the owner, Mary Martin-Line. She would transcribe them, and I would take them back to the business. This made me familiar with catching buses, El trains and walking to various high-rise offices in the Chicago business center commonly called the "Loop." My Aunt Fannie Watts, who was a custodial worker in that building, got me that job. She stressed honesty and said I might get good tips if I just treated the business people right. But that did not work all the time ---some of them were too thrifty (cheap).

  I continued my part time job in the Loop for a year and a half. High school demanded that I have more money, so I transitioned to a full-time job in a plastic factory. My older brother was working there, so since I was almost 17, I was able to get a job there too.

  Because of my work obligations, I never played sports after school. During regular school hours, I played the intramural stuff because you had to take gym and play a little of this and that, however, being on a team just was not a realistic possibility, because I was never available for necessary practice. Plus, I did not weigh much, and I was not that tall. I have to admit, I just wasn't athletic material that coaches wanted back in those days. The importance of studies didn't seem as important to me at that time, because I felt that I would be okay as long as I was able to work, (tragic, but true.) That discipline and training in good sportsmanship that comes with school-sponsored sports activities was something I needed.

High school became a greater challenge for me because of other factors in the environment that I could not fully understand or come to grips with at that time. The most devastating was a problem in my home. My parents separated and later divorced, so I was commuting back and forth between my Mom's house on the North side, where I was registered in school, and my Dad's house on the West Side. I continued to attend Waller High School. On the Near North Side, but I transferred to David G. Farragut H.S. on the West Side. I graduated from Farragut. During my first fourteen years of life, I did not know much of anything about racism, not to mention institutional racism. We had friends and associates in grammar school, but we normally studied in school and played as neighborhood youth at the local after school facilities. It was a different experience at both Farragut and Waller, and I encountered racism at both schools.

At Waller High School, which is where many of my friends from Manierre attended, you knew you were out of the familiar hood. You had to walk through enclaves of ethnicity to get there. It was my first introduction to what happens when little gangs begin to form. There were white gangs. I remember some of the names, the Cleveland Aces and the Deuces. These guys, 17 years and over, were teaching the 13 to 15 year –olds in their families to go to war with Blacks—so we had some pretty interesting run-ins at Waller High School.

Arnold was the grade school down the street from Waller high school that opened for high school make-up classes during the summer vacation season. Instead of using the high schools in the areas closest to the students' homes, Chicago Public Schools would require Black students, who lived as much as three to five miles away from the school to walk through a number of ethnic communities during those several weeks to attend classes. For the Black kids who did not live on my block, this truly was strange territory. These students were the ones who attended predominantly Black grade schools normally. As a result, this was my introduction to serious racial confrontations with young white teenagers. On the last day of summer school, a huge fight took place at Arnold Elementary school. Older brothers of both the Blacks and the whites got involved. Fortunately, the weapons were limited to bicycle chains, a few baseball bats and bare knuckles. Luckily, guns and drugs had not been introduced to either group at that time.

In 1955, I officially transferred to Farragut from Waller. At that time, the West Side Douglas Park area, as we called it, was the new territory for Blacks migrating from the Near North Side. The whole community, now called "Greater Lawndale" was transforming from Jewish to African-American. Two tragic murders appeared in the local news during that time. Emmet Till, from Chicago was murdered in Money Mississippi, and a seventeen-year-old Black student from Farragut named Alvin Palmer was murdered on his way back home on the south side. Parker reportedly was waiting for a bus at 55th and Kedzie where he was beaten to death with a hammer and other weapons, while surrounded by a mob of young white gang members. Chicago's racial boundaries at that time, made it extremely dangerous for Blacks to be in that area of the city. A young Black on the bus stop alone was defenseless. That occurrence in 1957 triggered a series of racial incidents at and around the high school.

Farragut at that time was less than 10 percent Black, with a lesser number of Latinos. The majority of the community at and around the school was ethnic white. It gradually became predominantly Latino, as it is today. My academics suffered because of my chosen priorities. I began to have loose affiliations with what we considered social clubs, later labeled as gangs. In other words, these affiliations gave me a day-to-day presence with activities that were designing my social development. I found myself vying for acceptance into the circles of some progressive guys who learned to respect how and when to fight in defense of reputation and street codes of conduct.

The typical rules were based on principles of respect for each other's family members, for the sweaters and jackets of each other's running buddies, and always for the elders of the community. Individuals who moved into the community from the outside generally learned from their new neighbors about the rules of fair play. Bullies and non-compliant newcomers usually met with daily problems from the vanguard that had been groomed by the elders who established the rules of neighborhood survival that we were all subjected to.

Because I always had an after-school job, I escaped many of the situations that came with just growing up in a struggling environment. At Farragut, I had limited social time and my daily routine kept me away from organized school-sponsored sports, just as it did at Waller High School. In some ways also, not going to certain locations travelling to and from large after-school related events kept me out of more serious trouble that so many of my friends ended up getting into. I always had a little money coming each payday. To quote a friend's philosophy, "If <u>you have a little money each day, you keep the money demon away."</u> Lack of any money and other inevitable temptations can be problematic for developing young people.

Not only did my jobs keep me out of serious trouble, but also I was fortunate enough to meet my high school sweetheart, Carol Randall at Farragut High School in the fall of 1956. We were introduced by Bessie Cubie, one of Carol's close friends, who lived across the street from me in the 1800 block of South Avers Avenue. Farragut was loaded with attractive, smart female students from my new Black side of Chicago. This cute, neatly dressed, classy young lady named Carol seemed to be the least interested in my advances. She became one of my main objectives. I pulled out all stops. I received her class schedule from sources in the school network. You would have to be in it to know how it worked I enrolled in her English class and got the same lunch period that she had. I worked from there to get my invite to meet her parents, siblings and the family pet dog, Juno. We found out a lot about each other from then on. We visited back and forth to each other's homes frequently for the remainder of high school. Carol was a needed positive influence on me. Her friendship and respect kept me out of a lot of trouble. She was one of the reasons I kept a full time job during high school. In those times, if you didn't have money to take your girl to a movie theater, you were in bad shape. I didn't have a car, but I had the bus fare. I always wanted to take her to inexpensive places that we both enjoyed and always wanted to be able to afford a theater and a snack.

We enjoyed bus rides from the west side to the north side or south side. We had family and friends who lived on all sides of town. Youthful rivals were coming from the four predominantly Black portions of the city. There have been several books written recently about street gangs in Chicago, some more accurate than others. But those of us who have lived in this city before and since the 1940's bear witness to the fact that the families who struggled to survive the racism and organized oppression learned to play by some home grown and self-enforced rules that are sorely needed in cities like Chicago today. I can recall a few names of the groups that interacted with each other with a certain level of dignity and respect as a self-imposed rule. It didn't matter whether or not they were engaged in competitive sports, or sharing the dance floor or skating rink with each other; our lady friends, sisters or young wives were to be respected at all times.

There were street boundaries that were established for the most part based on where you attended school or frequented well-known locations for entertainment or recreational purposes. You had bragging rights for good things like your school's athletic teams, your park district's facilities and for games and swimming pools, as well as for theaters and dancehalls in your neighborhood. Stores that kept up with fashions and trends, large churches known for community activities that helped celebrate holidays like Thanksgiving and Christmas, were all part of the good things we bragged about in our respective communities.

As those in my age group began to become adults, you could notice the harbingers to the new street organizations of today that would replace the entity that had been mostly athletic in nature. There had always been occasional small skirmishes that usually didn't amount to much. Once an altercation concluded, everyone knew it was over. There was no room for retaliation or revenge with violence. A tragedy took place while I was in my 2nd year of high school. A 15 –year- old kid was stabbed to death at a house party, a little Friday night social. The guy who went to prison for the killing grew up on the north side a few doors from me. He had moved to the Westside about the same time I did in 1955, but soon acquired a reputation for aggressive violence in his new neighborhood. After coming out of the Sheridan Youth Center in Illinois at age 17, his life began a downward spiral. He had been one of the many in our childhood group who cared about others. We talked many times over the years as boys growing up. We all knew the streets and its temptations and traps. At barely 17 years of age, he had a made up mind. By the time the two grandparents who raised him, both of whom I knew well, went to their graves, nothing that had been said or tried was able to reverse the deadly cycle that consumed his life. That was the beginning of the hard weapon involvement. The street that I lived on was just beginning to become threatening in terms of teenage violence and young gang violence in a real way. Organized crime was releasing guns and drugs into urban America. Chicago was no exception.

My last year of high school was both tough and revealing to me. In spite of my determination to graduate at all costs, I managed to get myself suspended because I got into a fistfight with one of the newly transferred football players who came to the school as a member of one of the newer street gangs. He knew I was a senior about to graduate, but he was unaware of our established rules of respect. He got involved in my illegal crap game that went on near the rear exit of the school store during lunch hour. On that day, I was overseeing our friendly game. A small select group of us had done this often for the past few years. This activity was allowed to go on, problem free all that time because we never argued or fought amongst ourselves. Every player knew the rule was to win or lose gracefully.

This young athlete had transferred to Farragut to play football. He brought his bad habit of bullying with him. We had words about his language and loud cussing. He had argued with another guy in the game, but he chose me to fight. I think it was because I was 5'10 and weighed all of 143 lbs. He was taller and heavier, but he wasn't used to fighting a smaller guy that didn't like bullies. I was dressed up in a suit that day because of the dress rehearsal for our well-planned graduation stage play that was scheduled to happen two days later. Two of my classmates, Chester Bell, first-string varsity football defensive tackle and Ernie Terrell (now deceased) who later turned professional, were staging a heavyweight championship bout for the school's graduation talent show. Carol Randall, Della Adams and Janice Brazil served as costume-dressed dancers in the show. These students, as adults, became lifelong friends to Carol and me.

    To this day I believe that my opponent might have won the fight if he hadn't ripped the pocket of my hard-earned, oversized, bought on credit, Robert Hall Sunday go to meeting suit. I became so incensed that I punched him in both his eyes almost at the same time. As a result, he had two serious black eyes. Not only was he a little shocked, he was also embarrassed. Besides being bigger than I was, he was a trained athlete as well.

    I was warned that some of his friends were waiting by the regular exit to get me after school. Being the diplomatic coward that I could be, I went out of another door on the back side of the school and caught the bus to work. My girlfriend Carol told me later that evening that when he saw her, thinking she was waiting for me to come out of the building; he questioned her, "Where is your boy?" Carol replied, "What boy are you talking about?" He lowered his sunglasses to show her his eyes, saying "The boy that did this." She said, "It looks more like a man did that, not a boy!" I always knew that she was the braver of us two. At my request, the regular guys from our group of friends, including Ernie Terrell, the local boy turned professional prizefighter, saw to it that she got home. We had followed that routine for several years. Usually, most of the Black students from our hood walked in the same direction practically every school day. This was the practice of thousands of other students, wherever they went to a school outside of the racial boundaries. We did this for social and safety reasons. By that time, I had learned that his name was Alonzo, although I did not see him for several more months. I had forgotten that this person was in the world.

Then, lo and behold! I'm walking through Douglas Park with Carol on a nice evening, in the summer of 1959. It was just about dusk dark. I saw the guy who had not forgotten the black eyes. He was with a small group of about four or five guys. They were sitting and standing around a bench. By the time I spotted my problem, it was too late; we were right in front of them. I was too close to turn around abruptly without bringing attention to us. I turned my head towards Carol, who was holding on to my right arm. I tried to block her face with the back of my head, hoping he would not see either of our faces. Oh boy, Alonzo did see me and called my name as we passed by them. My heart went straight to my throat as I tried to answer with some sort of growl. I whispered for Carol to walk on away. Her home was two blocks away, and I told her to go there quickly and tell her older brother what was happening. Being the little west side sister with great spirit, she whispers back, "I'm not going anywhere!" My mind is racing at this point. The rule of the game is don't show any fear. So now, I'm just praying. My fear was suddenly over powered by what I was seeing. I, almost instantly became more concerned about one of the guys in the group who kept eyeballing my lady with open lust. Out of somewhere came a totally different spirit in me.

I answered the one who had called my name as strongly as I could. As they surrounded us, I somehow managed to utter, "I see that you have your crew with you." I had not yet realized that one of his mob and I were pretty cool with each other from playing on the same sandlot softball team from time to time. We also had worn the same type of club sweater when we were younger. I know I was being guided by a force that confirmed for me, that there is a God in my life. From somewhere in my mind,

I found the words to blurt out, "If you want to get even from our fight, why don't you and I meet this coming Monday near Howland School after I get off work around 6 pm?" Howland was a popular neighborhood schoolyard hangout during summer evenings. My life-saving, "angel of the day", that I knew from the past, weighed in saying, "I believe that Howard will show if he says he will". My bully opponent agreed. As we walked away in opposite directions, I told Carol, "As soon as we get past this clump of bushes we will walk a little faster in case they have a mind change."

As expected, I never saw my opponent again. However, I did see my friend, Otis, my "guardian angel" (GA) again. By that time, I was back from a tour of active duty in the military. He told me that Alonzo happened to be a first cousin to another very good friend of mine, Alex, who lived just a few doors from me in the 1800 block of Avers. Otis went on to tell me that my young opponent was presently experiencing some very serious health problems, due to alcohol and drug abuse. I eventually started praying for a man that might have become a good friend had we met under better circumstances. That was a valuable spiritual lesson for me. I'm sure that stories like this are not unknown amongst my peers.

As I look back over all that happened to me in high school, I feel blessed to know that I made it through with nothing worse taking place.

I spent an extra semester in school because my main subject was w-o-r-k. I was actually working full-time from 4:00 p.m. until midnight during my last year of school. Some wanted to believe that I worked at the school because I attended there for so long. The real story is that I caught a bus two blocks from the school at the end of class and went downtown to Able Molding Company, where I worked as a Punch Press Operator from 4:00 pm to 12 midnight Monday thru Friday. My duties included being responsible for pick-ups and deliveries, doing inventory, and supervising the night crew.

My high school graduation was nowhere near the great celebration that my grade school graduation had been. As matter of fact, I never actually marched in the graduation. I received my diploma separately from my class because of my thirty-day suspension for fighting as a senior and bringing discredit to my class. I had to complete some other class work requirements, and I deserved the punishment rendered to me. I grew a little bit in character after it was all over.

During the 60's and 70's young men were coming back home from Illinois juvenile facilities where gang recruiting was flourishing. Professors Lance Williams and Benneth Lee at Jacob Caruthers Center for Inner City Studies have great knowledge of this history. In my generation, most young group members had learned to live by self-made rules that flew in the face of old school community laws that existed in the histories of most communities. As early as the mid and late 1950's, we had loosely organized gangs coming into existence from every side of town where struggling Blacks lived. The gangs were the Chaplains Sr. and Jr., the Clovers Sr. and Jr. and the Imperial Chaplains. About that time, the local and some federal politicians began to build high- rise buildings and move families from where they were living by community survival rules to new locations. This was done without any regard for the kinds of compounded social problems that were created for those already underserved households. The Democratic and Republican parties were the powers behind the movers and shakers.

My school life and my home life in those early years had challenges, but they were loaded with many positive factors. Although my parents separated, and my mother eventually remarried years later, I can say that I received love and discipline from both of my parents, along with the benefit of having two places to call home. I have so much compassion for children who grow up without two loving parents. I can understand with great humility what the father figure can mean to a child, especially boys who are very limited without ever knowing the guidance so desperately needed in times such as these we live in today. To have the memories available throughout one's lifetime is priceless. As I travelled back and forth from the West Side to the North Side, I dreamed and planned for the future.

The summer of 1959, after graduation, was one that Carol and I would cherish for the rest of our lives, mainly because it would be the last summer we would spend in Chicago, for a spell.

My father's big questions concerning me were: "What are you going to do?" "What are your plans?" I had one aunt, his only sister, who was pushing me to go to college and encouraging me from the standpoint of, "I'll help pay for it." The inner me was saying, "I must go to the Military. I have to go and meet the world. Let me go and join the Army."

Two incidents involving my father's pistol and me occurred during that time.

The first occurred the previous summer, in 1958, at a popular drive-up hotdog stand, located near Lake Street and Francisco Street on the near Westside of Chicago.

A group of twenty or thirty teenagers were eating sandwiches and drinking soda pop on a Thursday summer evening underneath the Lake Street El tracks. This had become a routine for some of us who would go to an indoor skating rink in Maywood, which was located a few miles west of Chicago and consisted of a smaller community of Blacks. On that particular night, a carload of males pulled up with music playing loudly and acting as if they were trying to make trouble with some of our little click that usually stood near each other whenever we were among people outside of our regulars. When it became obvious that these bully type fellows were actually trying to start a fight, I pulled my pistol from under my shirt and pointed it in plain view at the ground and sort of waved goodbye with my left hand. The group that was closest to the bullies started moving away from them. They got back into their convertible and left the area without uttering a word. That was the first time and last time any of my friends saw me with a gun in my hand. Only Dunigan and Carol knew that on occasion I might be packing.

The second time was truly my awakening. I had finished my 4 to 12--midnight shift at a plastic factory that I was working at a few miles from my home. Having just graduated from high school, I was undecided about my next move in life. The bus that I would take home from work passed by Carol's house on Ogden Avenue. That summer night Carol was standing at the window. We saw each other and that was my signal to get off the bus, which stopped a few yards from her front door, go kiss my girlfriend goodnight and walk about five blocks to my house. At about 1:30 am I am now two blocks from home, walking alone. An unmarked police car, with two detectives pulled up beside me. They both got out of the car. One asked me questions while the other one searched me. I had the pistol tightly placed inside my jockey shorts. In those days, the police searched a little differently than they do now. This officer brought both of his hands on both sides of my legs, but avoided touching me directly in the crouch area. Once again, my spirit calmed as I prayed silently while pulling out my credentials. My draft card and my school picture ID matched with my home address. My explanation about where I was coming from and where I was heading satisfied them and they went about their business and allowed me to go about mine.

That incident was a turning point for me in terms of flirting with incarceration or worse by carrying a gun illegally. My greater fear was the thought of breaking my father's heart by being arrested with his pistol that I had sneaked behind his back to obtain. That December of 1959, I was able to answer his question of "what was my plan" now that I had graduated from high school at the ripe old age of eighteen. "I will be the first of your sons to volunteer for military service." He was pleased and I was relieved. I thank God every day for allowing me to make that decision as a free man in a city where the likelihood of incarceration for a man my age was very possible. I graduated during the summer and got a new factory job at a chemical factory. I just skipped college altogether. I didn't even talk about college anymore. I concluded, that if I was not preparing for those entrance exams in my senior year, what was I going to look like trying to become a freshman in anybody's college or university? My journey toward manhood continued to teach me many tough lessons. Those experiences have helped to shape one of my philosophies of life. "To thine own self be true."

CHAPTER 3

MILITARY SERVICE & MARRIAGE

Duty to My Country and to My City: It was just a rude awakening. The first few months let you know that you had to make some decisions, and you had to come to grips with whether or not you were going to be a responsible person. I was introduced to the disciplinary system very early, and it was helpful.

My friend, Charles L. Dunigan and I, along with two other friends, joined the U.S. Army on a so-called Buddy Plan in December of 1959. We were together long enough to leave the Recruiting Station. We were split up from one another as soon as we were processed and issued uniforms at Fort Leonard Wood, Missouri. I did not see him for three years except when we came home from Basic Training. That was the year Charles and I got married to our childhood sweethearts. Charles married Bessie Cubie ten days before the Randall-Saffold marriage.

Carol and I got married in March of that year. Both of our parents had petitioned us to wait until I finished my active-duty obligations. However, these two 19- year olds, both born in the same year, same month and birthday's only two days apart, had made up their minds on the matter. Carol's parents, Ralph and

Ernestine Randall, become my beloved second set of parents, and I became as close to Carol's four as I was to my own six siblings.

The elders went along with our plan for Carol to stay at home with her parents for the few months it would take me to finish the next phases of training and receive my assignment to a permanent U. S. Army facility (post).

It took almost an entire year for us to get stabilized. She caught up with me in South Carolina for a short time, but it was difficult to make any long-term plans as I was being transferred from one post to another. Because of my low military pay grade, we were not entitled to what they called separate rations or additional money to help pay rent and buy food from the military compound.

My transfers were related to training that would give me a permanent MOS (Military Occupational Status). Each time my post changed, Carol would go back home and wait until I was clear; then we would once again try to stay together.

I was what they called "RA, Regular Army." I was very naïve about what that meant. I did not see my friends who I had signed up with on the so-called Buddy Plan for three years. They tricked me, oh yeah, they tricked me big time. They told me, you know, "Be all you can be" or whatever the slogan was in those days. Think about a guy coming off a block in Chicago to Fort Leonard Wood, Missouri, which was my first stop. But that was a very short stop, when I traded my grey Fedora and top coat for an olive-colored military uniform. My basic training was at Fort Hood, Texas. There might have been about two or three African-Americans in my company, and they were not country boys, they were from cities. Most of the white guys were country boys. They were Southerners. The few white recruits that came from the same cities the northern blacks came from, gravitated toward the blacks, socially.

This was the beginning of a real experience. I must have had a fight every other day about something that had to do with race or about being a new recruit in the Army. It was interesting and challenging to be a guy from the city who came to the table, headstrong and naïve about what the Military could do with your freedom. It was a rude awakening. This was in the early 1960's when the integration policy was only a few years old. Being introduced to the disciplinary system very early was helpful in the long run. But the initial shock was like, what have I gotten myself into? I soon learned to assume responsibility. Stationed at Fort Hood, Texas, I was made a Squad Leader of a small team of new soldiers from different parts of the Midwest as well as an attachment of Puerto Rican National Guard young recruits taking their required active military basic training. That overall experience was a very rich cultural and social exchange training opportunity that I will cherish forever.

From Fort Hood, I went to Fort Gordon, Georgia. My military classification test scores had landed me in the field of communications. Some of the training included becoming a lineman, which had to do with pole climbing, and attaching telephone wires, and the part I was assigned to had to do with radio and teletype, operating Morse code, and other field operations type things. It turned out that I would be sent to Fort Jackson South Carolina later and finally to Fort Harrison Indiana to be trained as a personnel administrative specialist.

That job classification, known in the Army as my Military Occupational Status (MOS) would be the deciding factor for how the United States government would use my skills to complete my tour of active duty. Subsequently I then got an assignment to Fort Belvoir, Virginia for the last 18 months of my three-year term. I was able to bring Carol to live off post by this time. We lived in Washington, D.C., and I made the 20-mile commute back and forth to the post by car or bus. Carol got a job at a hospital there in D.C. She was just beginning her nursing career. The future started looking bright for us.

Just before I got out of the Army, I applied for the Metropolitan Police Department in Washington, D.C. I was getting used to Washington, D.C., and I had about 120 days left in the Military. They had announced a Police Exam. After I passed the written exam with flying colors, I began to get correspondence from the

Police Department, taking me from Phase A to Phase B. Finally, on the Post where I was stationed, the big talk was "You know Saffold is gonna be the police in town. We can't go to D.C. no more. This guy is gonna be there, you know."

That was my first introduction to discrimination in the Police Department. I took the physical exam, and the guy told me that I did not have six natural or filled molars. Now, the Army had done so much dental work on me that I thought I almost had a false tongue. They had pulled half my teeth and replaced them. But the D.C. Police Department wanted me to have six natural or filled molars. The guy who told me this, kind of reminded me of Gomer Pyle, but he was the police. I said," I'd like to see that in writing." I wasn't applying for the K-9 Unit, so I was indignant. I was upset because I had gotten in the 90 percentile in terms of the written exam. Because of my job in Clerical Administrative work, I was steeped in reading rules and regulations. Test taking was easy for me because I was giving tests to other people. The long and short of it is that they sent me a very disappointing rejection letter saying, "You didn't pass the physical." I was down to about 30 days when I received that notification. Up until that point, we were sure we would remain living in D.C., at least for a while.

I was considering re-enlistment, but Carol said, "Let's go home. If you want to go back in after a year, I would be okay with that." My friends on active duty went straight into the Vietnam War. I am sure I would have gone as well.

As a child living in public housing, Carol dreamed of becoming a nurse. From high school to City College to Licensed Practical Nurse, to Registered Nurse, she pursued her dream. As the years passed, she worked at various hospitals, clinics and nursing facilities. Attending special classes and seminars was embedded in her heart. She was determined to learn to teach others what she was learning. Her last part time job, after retiring, was at Triton College, located in the western suburbs of Chicago. Carol joined the faculty team in the department of nursing. She loved teaching students from the surrounding communities, including Maywood and Bellwood, Illinois where the struggles of day-to-day survival confronted many of the students.

Carol was determined to mentor and nurture her students until she was certain that they understood the ethics and pride that came with that honorable profession. The youthfully inspired journey for the two of us lasted fifty-six years.

After experiencing life's interruptions, as seniors in our sixties and early seventies, Carol and I treasured the ability to reflect on the many times each of us had experienced having our heart broken and mended only to have it broken and mended again. During that period, we had buried each of our parents, four of my siblings and three of hers and before any of those losses occurred, we had experienced the loss of our son, Howard Saffold, Jr. in 1963.

Our faith in God grew as we learned more about how to trust the will of the Creator of all humankind.

In June of 2014, Carol was told she had contracted cancer of the pancreas and it was spreading. After fighting back with all that was available in the medical arena, my friend for life succumbed to that dreadful disease on November 8, 2016.

She made sure that I mailed her ballot in plenty of time to have it counted in that historically significant election. Unfortunately, Hillary Clinton lost to Donald Trump.

CHAPTER 4

BECOMING A COP

I got out of the service in late December of 1962. After a few attempts I still had found no work in Washington, D.C., so we decided to come back to Chicago. Making a career of the Military was not a desire for either of us, so we opted to return to civilian life. We were not financially prepared for coming back home because we did not have very much of a nest egg. My first job was at the Veterans Administration, initially as a personnel clerk. Next was the Chicago Transit Authority (CTA). Where I drove what they called a rapid transit (an elevated train) as a motorman, conductor, and switchman. That job lasted a year and a half. I had been well-trained, enjoyed the work and I liked my hours. Unfortunately, a tragedy came to our little family that changed the situation. Our baby son died. I had already been scheduled to report for work in what turned out to be just two hours after his death. I called my job from the hospital emergency room to tell the scheduling clerk what had happened. His response was, "There's nothing with you is it?" It took me for a loop. I was momentarily shocked. I don't remember saying anything, not even hanging up the phone. Eventually the station superintendent or someone who was a little more prepared to deal with employees than the clerk was, called to offer his condolences and explain the procedure for taking time off for death in the family. But this was an early warning to me. I knew that I felt a lot differently about my place of employment after that day. Not too many months later, I applied, took a test and was hired by the Chicago Police Department.

I did not know much about the Police Department, but I knew some older men who had been police officers for many years. As a youngster, I had run-ins with some of the neighborhood police officers. When I say run-ins, those are the things that you get into when you're young, gambling on the street, absent from school, being places you don't need to be during school hours, and those kinds of things. In spite of that, I had a lot of respect for the Black police officers that I did know. One in particular was Officer Russell, who lived about six doors from my house. When I was a kid, I would see him going back and forth to work in his uniform. He worked out of the station that was near the school I attended. His wife was a very nice lady who would send me to the store regularly. Those few pennies and nickels a day kept candy coming my way.

During that time, another police officer who stands out in my memory is Officer Ray. My father would drop him off at the police station where he worked, when we were on our way to sell Fuller Products. He and my father were close friends, and I had a lot of respect for him.

There was publicized recruitment for Black officers during the time in which I was hired. I later realized that I was one of the fortunate ones who was not classified as having a heart murmur or flat feet. I provided a list of people as references, including a couple of police officers. One elected official told me to let him know if I had any trouble. However, I did not have any trouble and did not have to get political help.

We had 18 weeks of training back then. Best that I can remember, it had a lot to do with learning the Illinois revised criminal statutes, city ordinances, physical training defensive tactics, weekly written exams, and firearm training. The training also included how to use the baton and hand cuffs.

In my class, there were about six African Americans out of 30 people. There was a new superintendent of police. For the first time in the history of Chicago, they had hired an individual from outside the police department, a criminologist who did not have a law enforcement background, Orlando Wilson. O.W. Wilson was nearing the end of his tenure by the time I came to the job. Part of his mandate had been to bring more minorities into the police department and create a new image to include renewed public trust after the famous Summerdale scandal. Police corruption and racial discrimination towards Blacks is a widely discussed topic, and a subject of many books, articles, news reports, research reports, op-eds and editorials. Coming on this job in the mid-sixties was an opportunity to see a lot first hand and to be involved in doing a lot to change things, as you will see reading forward.

The civil rights movement of the 60's was beginning to become a common discussion in urban America, and Chicago was no exception. The conspicuous absence of Blacks on the job was beginning to be spoken to by civil rights organizations and church leaders. On a national level, the Black politicians also had begun to get pressure from the civil rights movement to hire more Blacks in the police departments around the country. We were all direct benefactors of that thrust.

In this process of change, there had been a merger between the Chicago Park District Police Department and the Chicago Police Department. That greatly increased the percentage of African Americans in the department. No hiring of this magnitude has ever equaled that of the 1964-1965 hiring of African Americans since that time. The hiring of African Americans by the Chicago Police Department has returned to the dismal numbers reflected in the 1940's and 1950's. Blacks have now been buried in a sea of people called minorities. They did that little window of hiring in Chicago, and then it just ceased after the 1965 group was in place, until the AAPL law suit.

The changes did not take place without the use of the court system. As a leader in AAPL, I was before the courts many times on both sides of the law—as a defendant in a criminal case and as a plaintiff in the civil cases.

CHAPTER 5

A SECOND RUDE AWAKENING

I had little knowledge of the big picture of some aspects of how the Chicago Police Department operates. I did not socialize with police officers on any regular bases. I only knew two Black officers on the North Side and two on the West Side, while still in my teens. That was it. I knew them, and they knew us as neighborhood children. In terms of discrimination and brutality, I was very naïve. I thought I had left all of the bigotry and racial confrontations in the Military. I was soon to learn that I had slept through some major issues in Chicago. My first conscientious wake up came, I'm sad to admit, during the mid – 1960's. I had become accustomed to dealing with my personal challenges as they came to me. I finally saw what many others probably had seen and maybe had experienced in earlier years.

In 1966, I was a rookie with less than a year on the job when Chicago became involved in civil disturbances in both the African American community and in the Latino community. I'm talking about the time of the first marches into Marquette Park when Dr. King first came to town. I was nearly three years into my career when much of urban America felt the backlash of Dr. Martin Luther King Jr's assassination. By me working in the predominately white community, I did not see the overt display of police abuse, prior to and during that time that produced an entity made up of Black police officers who had recently been hired in the Chicago Police Department (CDP).

In the beginning stages of organizing the Black police officers in Chicago, it became very obvious to me that prior to the creation of the group that called themselves the Afro-American Patrolman's League (AAPL) there were other groups that had been in existence for a number of years including the Guardians of Chicago. These groups were well known to their respective communities as well as the police department that employed them. Their purposes for existing varied from city to city. Many of them had realized the impact of racial discrimination against them as officers and members of their families and communities. There are limited records of how this problem was being addressed from one city to the next, but there was no record of a concerted effort to address this problem being put forth prior to the late 1960's. I joined the AAPL in 1968 when it was in its embryonic stage of constructing its board of directors. I became a board member and the vice-president in charge of recruitment in that same year. I had been a police officer for three years by the time this group came into existence. The personalities of the men that made up this group ranged from downright ghetto brothers from the hood to the conservative middle class Black and everything in between. The size of the group fluctuated between eight and fifteen depending on the temperature in the meeting room or the amount of heat that one might feel from the police department hierarchy. The Chicago Police Department policy makers realized early on that these young Black officers were going to be more difficult to manipulate than their predecessors. The stated goals were bold and challenging. Our speeches were laced with "we're going to improve the relationship between the police department as an institution and the Black community." The historical relationship was one of distrust, brutal treatment, double standards of service and protection and some of the most vicious being Blacks who took pride in showing their white bosses and co-workers how insensitive they could be.

We also stated in our public forums "we wanted to improve the relationship between white and Black police officers." The reader should keep in mind that we're talking in an atmosphere of civil unrest. Dr. Martin Luther King Jr. had just been assassinated. Black communities all over the country were experiencing riots or feeling the tension of the possibility of one occurring. Race discussions were considered a no-no in the police squad rooms where all officers get their daily assignments before going on patrol.

The issues of day-to-day crime fighting were very carefully touched on by the supervisory personnel, so as not to evoke any race-based attitudes that the individual may be harboring. Our third overall objective was what we called "total police reform." We believed that the police officer possessed too much discretionary power to be overseen by other police only. There needed to be an independent investigative agency to monitor complaints of police misconduct. Police reform became the center piece of the League's activity. It would consume the vast majority of our time and resources over the two decades. The various programs and activities will be addressed in detail in later chapters.

From day one of my involvement with the League, the issue of race became such a challenge to our overall reasons for existing that we decided to confront it head on. The AAPL sponsored an educational seminar for the purpose of having some open dialogue between white and Black police officers. After much debate about where the white officers might feel comfortable, we chose the University of Chicago as a site. We scheduled the sessions to take place on Sundays so as to get maximum participation from those who might have difficulty getting time off on the busier days of the week. The invitations were extended to the white officers first. Our rationale was that the discussion would go more smoothly if there were a minimum amount of confrontation posed for either group. In the first instance, we would be able to address the issues more thoroughly once both groups had a chance to express their concerns while talking among themselves.

The turnout was not as great as we had hoped, however, fifty or so attended the first session. The theme was centered on the issue of "Why do you think the relationship between the Black community and the police is so negative?" There was one young white officer in attendance that had recently obtained a degree in sociology and decided to put his teaching into practice by joining the Chicago Police Department. His stated reason for attending the seminar was to gain insight into why people in the Black community resented him so much. He expressed the feeling of total rejection even in non-confrontational situations. The concerns expressed by this young officer pretty much summed up the concerns of most of the people in that room. He wanted to know what kinds of things could lead to such open hostility and resentment. And more importantly, he wanted to know what could be done to rectify this potentially dangerous situation. The candor used in asking his questions and sharing his views lifted the heavy air inside this mall conference room. This session ended on a positive note that seemed to indicate that we were on the right track to address the issue of race relations with Chicago Police officers, a task that the Department hierarchy had avoided without explanation over the years.

The events that followed that Sunday afternoon stand out in my mind as though they have occurred repeatedly, year after year since that early 1970 seminar. When we opened the doors of the conference room the following Sunday our attendance had dropped to just a few people. The word had reverberated throughout the department that to attend the workshops was the kiss of death. The young man that had been so assertive in the first session came to the door of the room and beckoned for me to come to where he was standing. He was nervous about even staying in the outside area too long. He said, "Officer Saffold, you won't believe what happened to me when I reported for work Sunday night." He went on to tell me that he had been approached by three different levels of the department before he got off work that night. The first being the shift commander. In a paramilitary organization this individual represents power and authority. This is the individual that everyone working on that shift takes their orders from. He (there were no she's in those days) represented a level of achievement that most of the personnel, especially the youngsters, dream of acquiring sometime during their career. He said to the young recruit, "Whose side are you on Kid? Has anyone told you who those guys are that organized that meeting? If you want to get along on my shift you better be more careful in choosing the type of meetings you attend."

The second contact came in the person of his immediate supervisor. This person decides what his evaluation report looks like when it is time to make a record for yourself for promotional and assignment purposes. This is the person that gets the first opportunity to recommend you for a meritorious citation or a disciplinary action. He said, "You are about to create a whole bunch of problems for yourself, Recruit. If you continue to look for trouble you'll be out of here on your ass so fast you won't know what hit you. You are working for a good commander and you don't want to piss him off."

The third approach came from a fellow officer. "The word is out that you are partial to the n***s," he said, "Let me give you a word of advice. You better choose your friends more carefully. You're working in a hot district. Friday and Saturday is cut and shoot night over here. Who are you going to call when you need back up? Some of the guys are saying they don't even want to have a beer with you after work."

The discussion between us went on for several minutes. We both concluded that he would be better off not coming back to participate in the rest of the sessions. The risk of being ostracized at work and after work for the police officer and the family can be devastating and dangerous. My story about this young recruit lays the foundation for much of the information that I intended to share about my experience with the Chicago Police Department and the Afro-American Patrolman's League.

From November 1965 to April 1968, I had witnessed enough incidents that had literally thrust me into the arms of the AAPL. I am forever grateful that the organization came along when it did. I had seen enough in less than three years on the job to send me packing out the door. In the training academy, I had witnessed several timid sponsored recruits become power drunk and vicious upon receiving only a few weeks of the gun and badge training. I had seen serious dedicated peace officers suppress their dignity and self-respect under the mere threat of being transferred out of an assignment they desired so they kept their mouths shut about any wrong doing. . I had seen lying scoundrels brag about their untouchable position because of who they knew. I had seen supervisory bosses look the other way while the rights of citizens were being trampled on, even when they were asked to intervene.

During my regular work routine, I encountered many different personalities and sickening turns in events. I recall a time while I was in recruit training on the west side at the Fillmore Station there was a recruit who was in training with me. He stated he hadn't been around any Black people in his life. This involved a prisoner in lock-up who seemed to be familiar with being in a jail. We were both busy, dressed in brown khaki uniforms learning procedures from the lock-up keeper. The guy in the cell asked for a baloney sandwich. My white co-worker gave it to him. An hour later, the guy said, "I want another sandwich." The new recruit said, "I can't give you but one." The guy called him vulgar names and threatened him. The recruit went over to the cell and gave the guy another sandwich. We got a chance to chat outside the lock up later during the shift. I told him that he was giving the guy the impression that he was afraid of him. He played it off as if he felt sorry for the man. We were in the same class for the remainder of the training weeks.

Shortly after graduation, I saw this same young recruit on the streets in full uniform with a firearm. He had turned from a very intimidated, scary kind of personality to a gruff, rough, blood and guts kind of guy shortly after they gave him that gun and badge. My concern compelled me to become very vigilant towards how officers react to people. I started to pay attention to how some white officers reacted to Black people and how Black officers reacted to white people. I watched arrest and non-arrest situations. I was concerned with how the training was being applied to the communities we worked in.

My Army experience helped me understand those types of behavior patterns. I knew my limitations relative to analyzing behaviors but that didn't stop me from paying attention. The Paramilitary/police arena when a person being addressed is not considered important enough to automatically be respected; the interaction can reveal a tone and temperament of the encounter very quickly.

Historically, the AAPL's effort to address community relations and white/Black police relations always got cut short when the discussion became heated. The possibility of a flare up always seemed to frighten the conveners if they were the policy makers who feared outbursts or confrontations. How tragic.

My first few years of police service gave me some very distinct impressions of how the best and worst practices looked. I began to notice how news articles and editorials that addressed opinions about or from elected officials seemed to encroach more and more on police discretion and decision making. New scandals rolling out in the media provoked inside talk about incidents where officers would express regret when they had to back off of a legitimate arrest because the person was a noted figure or one with a relationship to a politician, for me was who am I to criticize the powers that be? After a few seasons of GAGA, (go along to get along) there seemed to be no end in sight.

On the very first day that I reported to the Shakespeare Station, my district commander said that he was obligated to tell me that nobody wanted to work with me. He was blatant and said, "So we'll probably be changing your partner on a regular basis until you get familiar with the district. Then you'll be working by yourself for the most part." He was in a dilemma because my probation period was a year, and he did not want to get in trouble by having me work alone too soon. At the same time, he wanted me to know that officers assigned to this station were not used to having Black partners. My shift rotated every 30 days, so I got a chance to see the difference in how the police handled domestic disturbances in the home, lost or missing children, and school truancy in a predominately white community. It was an eye opener in terms of my learning the skills of being a police officer and a public servant where people respected the law.

The first time I saw serious physical brutality at the hands of a police officer was when I witnessed the beating of a Puerto Rican youth. My partner and I were chasing a 16-year-old kid who was driving a stolen car. He was driving, and I was a rookie. We were working the 4 PM to midnight shift. This kid drove around the same four-square blocks for about 10 minutes until squad cars finally boxed him in and he crashed into a storefront business that had closed for the night. The impact of the crash dumped him out of the front door onto the ground. Three or four cars that had responded to the radio alert came to the scene of the crash scene. Several officers pounced on this little five foot-three, 119- pound kid. They administered a serious leather glove-with-sand-in-the-knuckles beating. This was my first exposure to a cowardly gang type beating of anyone, by the police.

Since my partner and I had initiated the pursuit, standard policy dictated that we were responsible for the arrest and related paperwork. I was just learning to do police case reports, so I was being taught to carefully prepare the document that would go to the youth division and ultimately to juvenile court. The narrative had to exclude any reference to the beating. Officials purposely delayed the court appearance date to allow time for the youngster's wounds to heal.

I had not been assigned a permanent partner at that time but up until then the partner with me that night, who I had worked with a couple of times before, had been a very good resource in terms of sharing information and training tips. Therefore, I didn't hesitate to ask him, "Why the beating, man?" His unremorseful explanation was, "You have to get to them at this early point because you don't know how the case is gonna turn out in court. What you do know," he went on to say, "is that he will probably show up in court wearing a shirt and tie and be accompanied by his parents, a social worker and maybe even priest or something". So you make your impression on them upfront. You let them know that when they make us chase them in a car, they place the lives of the police and other innocent people in jeopardy. So, you teach them a lesson while you can." I realized that he was sincerely expressing his true belief that the police are justified in being the judge, jury, and the executioner on the street when we feel the need to be.

I took that lesson to heart for the remainder of my career. As time went on, I began to compare how Blacks policed young Black teenager with how their white counterpart functioned with Black teens under similar circumstances. We could learn and teach each other quite a bit in this profession, once we acknowledge the racial reality. The race of the teen made a big difference, especially when the officer puts human compassion back into the equation.

After my probationary period was completed, I received a permanent partner. This officer had finished his probation the same time I did. In contrast to the many negative events that I had encountered during that period, my new partner, presented a breath of fresh air at this critical time for me. His name was Bill G. He was my age, a former U.S. Marine and quite a decent character to work with: mild mannered, but he had no reservations about fighting, whenever challenged. But I never saw him go beyond using the necessary force to affect an arrest. What I appreciated about him most was that he had routinely and quickly responded to my radio assignments automatically when we both worked our one-man cars. Usually, his patrol beat was adjacent to mine whenever we worked the midnight shift or the day shift. The Shakespeare district was considered a medium crime community that could maximize manpower by using one-man cars on those two shifts.

Whenever we rotated to the much busier evening shift (3 to 11PM –or 4PM to midnight) we would try to get assigned to the same car. It was a no brainer for both of us. He was new to the district the same as I was. No fellow officers were jumping up and down to work with him, mostly because he actually enjoyed doing all aspects of day-to-day police work as much as I did. And no one wanted to work with the only Black guy in the mix either. It was a conversation that the two of us would have frequently, without any strain. We developed a friendship that lasted through the years.

The very last night that Bill G and I worked together was memorable for both of us. We got a chance to reflect on it occasionally years later. During that time the police squad radios were still in the car only. This particular night, when we came back to the squad car after a routine service call, the radio dispatcher directed us to go to the police station and told me to personally report to the Watch Commander alone.

When I got to the Watch Commander's office, he was sitting with a plain- clothed detective.

After introducing this person to me, the Commander said, "Howard, did you call Internal Affairs Division tonight?" My response was "No Sir, was I supposed to?" I wanted to know what made him ask the question. He went on to tell me why the detective was there. He was investigating an "anonymous" complaint that a supervising sergeant who was about to retire in two months had come on the police radio that night saying, "I'm chasing a male N-word and he just ran up the stairs to the Sheffield L station platform." The detective went on to say that I was being asked the question because I was the only Black officer working that night, he thought that I may have been offended enough to anonymously report this racial slur to Internal Affairs Division (IAD). The commander knew that retiring sergeant, Sergeant H, was not popular with some of the rank & file in that station because if you were caught not doing what you were supposed to do on his shift or you were caught someplace other than your assigned post, he would initiate disciplinary action against any and all violators. Some of those same type individuals also had distaste for me. So, this was a perfect opportunity to cause a problem for their favorite Black and one of their unpopular supervisors Sergeant H with one anonymous phone call.

After confirming that I did not make the call, my Watch Commander said, "Howard, we need you to do us a favor. We need you to write a report that indicates you've been working with and around the sergeant for over a year and never had any type personal problem racially with him. I told them I could do better than that. I said, "He possibly saved my life one night a few months ago."

I recounted the incident. I was working midnights in a one-man car, when I spotted a speeding vehicle with three young white men. The driver ran a red light and was speeding. I put my blue roof light on and turned my spotlight on his rear window but he wouldn't pull over. I called the squad operator and told him I was riding behind this traffic violator with my blue light on, and I wasn't chasing him because he was now going the speed limit, but he wouldn't stop. I gave his license plate number and a description of the vehicle over the air. After travelling several blocks, he finally stopped in front of a single-family house, and I gave that address. The two passengers jumped out of the car and went into that house. The driver began to follow them into the house. I reported that I was exiting my car to make an arrest. I shouted, "Stop now!" to the driver and he stopped. I asked to see his driver's license. He told me he didn't have to show me shit and started to walk away. I instinctively jumped on his back, grabbed him around his neck and choked him while pulling him backwards to the ground. At that time, it wasn't called a chokehold, it was just a takedown technique I had learned in training. I was not going to let him go until he submitted to me. He was pulling my forearm, which was underneath his Adam's apple. My drop to the ground from behind placed him bent into a half sitting posture and my weight would prevent him from getting up. My head was slightly down next to his so I couldn't see all of what was going on around me. Suddenly I heard the sergeant's familiar gravelly voice saying, "Where are you going with that shotgun?" I looked upward as best I could while holding my grip. The other two young men had gone into the house and come back out with an older man who was walking in front of them brandishing a shotgun. Sergeant H. who like everyone else that was on the Radio Band had heard my call on the radio and heard the address said, "That's my son he's holding!" the older guy shouted. Then I heard the sergeant again. "I don't give a damn who he is to you. If you don't get back into the house with that shotgun you're going to get shot." That's when I'm realizing vividly, "Negro, you're in the middle of the night on a shift by yourself." This all seemed to be in slow motion. The sergeant called for a squadron (Paddy wagon). It pulls up and this sergeant says "Help this man put handcuffs on this guy." Up until then the guys were walking around us casually like "Oh my. Wow! What's going on here?" They eventually helped put handcuffs on the guy. The Sergeant says, they'll take him from here. Before I knew I knew it I blurted out, "No, I'm going to take him to the station in my car." The station was only a few blocks away. He was in the back seat of my car, handcuffed. I felt a strong urge to do him some physical harm. I stopped the car and turned my head to look at him sitting on the back seat opposite me. After starring at for a few seconds, I calmed down. At that point, I could hear him in a childish, whining voice, saying things like his father had marched with Dr. Martin Luther King. My brief stare was saying "You are completely in my charge Junior, and I'm going to beat your butt with a pen." I charged him with speeding, resisting arrest, battery against a police officer and refusing to produce a driver's license. The judge found him guilty of not producing his license and fined him $5 and told me that I would have to file separate complaints for the other charges. No one from the state attorney's had filed any papers from my original case report. It was several months after the incident before the case had even come up in traffic court. I was told unofficially that this guy's family was politically connected.

Now, several months later, my superiors were asking me to write a support reference for Sergeant H., who that night had done what no one else had done by coming between me and immediate danger.

Side Bar Alert: A police investigation eventually discovered that at least two of those officers involved in the Puerto Rican youth's beating, plus three others in that police district, were cited as being card-carrying Ku Klux Klan members who only got discovered after they were transferred into a predominantly Black district on the West side of Chicago. According to news reports, one or two of them had physically abused a White gang member of the Simon City gang in that district. One supposedly struck the kid over the head with a baton (wooden club) with the center drilled out and a lead rod had been inserted in the hollowed space and resealed. Supposedly, the youngster who filed the report was a relative of a local elected official. The investigation resulted in several officers being transferred for punishment purposes to a predominately Black district on the West side of the city. As the investigation continued, their membership in the Klan became public knowledge

Here is the text of a newspaper article regarding the Police/Klan members:

"Chicago (UPI) 6 Chicago Policemen Linked to Klan Unit

A six-foot cross suitable for repeated burnings and an arsenal were taken Thursday from the home of a policeman who allegedly had formed a Ku Klux Klan cell made up of at least six city police officers. Police estimated upwards of 200,000 rounds of ammunition, much of it in bandoliers, live hand grenades and semiautomatic rifles were found in the home of Donald Health, 30. The KKK connections of Heath, a patrolman in a predominantly Negro West Side district, came to light when investigators noticed the three letters painted in small blocks on the rear deck of his private auto. Heath and three unidentified police Klansmen will be taken before the Police Review Board for dismissal action. Their membership in the organization, though it violates no law, violates department regulations. The other two policemen identified as members of the Klan resigned after disclosure of the ring Thursday. They were Richard Stanton, 33, who worked in the same district as Heath and Dennis Aloia, 25, a member of another predominantly Negro West Side district.

While Police Supt. James B. Conlish, Jr., revealed the existence of the organization at a news conference, Internal Inspection Division detectives who had been aided by the Cook County State's Attorney's office raided Heath's home. They said they found a six foot cross made of plastic and designed for repeated burnings; bandoliers of thousands of rounds of ammunition, live hand grenades later disarmed, a submachine gun, four automatic rifles, four 1 pistols, six knives, a gas mask, American and Confederate flags, white Klan sheets, hate literature and application blanks from the headquarters of the National Knights of the Ku Klux Klan in Tucker, GA. Authorities said the group's activities, which they described as in the planning stages, were discovered last summer and that the investigation intensified in the past few months.

Investigators said one policeman told his superiors he had been approached by one of the groups and asked to join. Capt. Raymond Clark, director of the ID, said the group of at least six policemen met in either Heath's home or in taverns but limited contacts with other KKK elements to letters or telephone. Conlish said the men also could be prosecuted in connection with the cache of weapons to be investigated by federal authorities. Conlish said Thursday he did not now know whether other members of the police department belonged to the small organization but said he did not believe it was widespread. He also said he did not think the weapons had been stolen. The police department has come under fire in recent months because of various scandals. Thursday, Mayor Richard J. Daley said 12 of the policemen assigned to the Chicago Transit Authority System to protect public transportation passengers against an outbreak of crime would be transferred to fight the growing crime wave in a South Side neighborhood where an Alderman was shot and wounded Tuesday night."

Back to my last night at the Shakespeare police station. I was being asked to write a reference to the fact that I had a good relationship with the man who possibly saved my life. I bargained I would write the report, "Contingent on you, commander transferring me out of here right now" I went on to explain, "You already have me in a situation where most of the time I don't have anyone I can count on to back me up when I'm working a one-man car, and now on the night I'm in a two-man car, this incident occurs. Neither my partner nor I heard the radio broadcast, and I am now accused of being a cowardly anonymous phone caller that reported it. You have to get me out of here because I don't feel like going through anything else in this district." They agreed and asked me where I would like to be transferred to. I told them the choice for me would be to go to Area 4 Task Force on the West side of the city. It is located in the middle of three Black districts and one predominantly Latino district. They agreed, contingent on me writing the report right then. I then asked to speak to Sergeant H. before writing my official report He came to the station. He was visibly shaking. I said, "Did you use that term Sergeant?" He said, "Howard, I wasn't talking about you, I was talking about a dog-ass N-word, not you." This man in his late sixties, I would guess used the N word in such a matter of fact way that I don't believe he saw anything wrong or out of the ordinary about using that word.

Soon after that, I was transferred to the Black community. The glaring difference in standard practices between the two communities literally jumps right out at anyone who is paying attention.

In spite of my perplexing experiences, I was able to do well and maintain a good record as a new officer.

Now, at the most unpredictable point in my police career, I had been transferred from the Northside to the Westside to a specialized unit they called the Task Force.

Historically, when the Chicago Police Department creates a specialized unit, its twofold purpose is to address some specific crime problem and to select the appropriate personnel to participate in the operation of that unit, to use one example. The Task Force that was in existence in the 1960's had a special mission to address problems in certain areas of the city. The assigned boundaries corresponded with the Detective areas, i.e.,

Area 1 (police districts 1, 2, 3 and 21); Area 1 (police districts 4, 5, 6 and 7 and so on.) The task force operated during hours that overlapped the normal shifts, i.e., 10 am to 6 pm and 6 pm to 2 am seven days a week. The unit was rated on its ability to generate arrests of any kind. However, great emphasis was placed on felony type arrests. The same communities that had been classified as "High Crime" areas were where most of the arrests were generated. These arrests were generated in several ways. Most common among them were what police refer to as "on view" which means the officers observed the incident as it was taking place or some person flagged the officers down to tell them about some crime that was being committed or they received a radio communication of a crime in progress. Making arrests and going to court were the two main functions of this type of unit and the individuals in these type units were generally perceived by other police personnel as necessary and usually helpful in situations that needed backup assistance or would be so time consuming to the regular patrol officer that he or she would gladly turn an arrest over to the task force officers. The selection process for this type of unit was traditional, somebody had to know somebody. Transfer requests were accepted as routine, however, a little help from the right person made the difference. The positive side of this kind of unit was it had a reputation for being able to generate very impressive arrests and statistics. This entity was later to be called special operations. The new name and the new focus began the process for the negative side of the ledger.

The command personnel for this specialized unit became a part of an elite group that generated the majority of the department's arrest statistics. The reports to the FBI, the media and the various units of the CPD reflected the justification (on paper) for street stops, mass arrests, court time and overtime. Performance ratings and special recognition became the foundation for promotions and expansion of operations (No existing report has ever shown the quantitative relevance of these thousands of arrests and their overall impact on crime and the quality of safety in these crime-ridden communities.)

Ultimately new turfs were created that allowed coteries to exist within the police department organizational structure. The operations bureau acquired add-ons such as Gang crimes north and south, public housing north and south, mass transit, school patrol, etc. The district commanders of the predominately Black and Latino communities where these extremely aggressive "arrest machines" were placed, had little if any control over the personnel assigned to these units. The day-to-day activities of these people had a direct impact on the citizens in those respective districts. Citizen complaints (especially youth) of verbal and physical abuse, unnecessary street stops, and vehicular searches were numerous and constant. Most of these complaints ended up being classified as not sustained, exonerated or unfounded year after year. So the supervisors of these units continued to climb the management ladder while most of its officers became the new first line supervisors within those units as well as the predominately Black and Latino districts that they were allowed to function in. The complaints from citizens going to the Office of Professional Standards and the police department's Internal Affairs Division exceed nine thousand annually. These numbers do not include the complaints that are refused from youth under the age of eighteen, or the people who have become frustrated by the investigative system's failures and simply do not bother to complain at all. Some estimates show these numbers to be greater than the reported incidents. How does this reality impact community police relations in these communities? There are reports available that have been tracking the police department's Chicago Alternative Policing Strategy (CAPS) for the past six years in every general term. These reports indicated the small number of officers who actively engage in or adhere to the concept of the program. And in more recent months, more and more citizens have stopped attending these meetings due to the lop-sided police dominance in the so-called partnership.

 One of the many trying periods I had as a police officer was when I had an unbelievable experience with a partner for the evening, whom I'll call Officer Joe. I had served as a beat officer in several stations around the city by the time I transferred back to the Grand Crossing police station. Officer Joe was careful to assure me that he was aware of my affiliation with the AAPL.

This encounter is not only relevant to police-community relations, but it also highlights how a lack of training and supervision can affect a police officer's attitude toward his co-workers as well as the public he serves. Working the midnight shift usually provides ample time for two police officers working in a patrol car to converse and exchange views. Generally, the midnight to 8:00 a.m. shift nerally, the midnight to 8:00 a.m. shift would compel the assigned officers to work together for a period of at least 30 days before they would rotate to a new shift, and perhaps a new partner.

On this particular occasion, I was working with a young White officer in his late twenties who had been a police officer for two years. At that time, I had been on the job approximately eight years. The AAPL was well into its fifth year and the issues of Black and White police and police community relations were daily discussions. Fights between Black and White police officers occurred in the police station with regularity. Incidents of police abuse appeared in the newspapers almost daily, reinforcing the fact that AAPL still had a long way to go with this portion of its objectives.

Officer Joe was careful to assure me that he was aware of my affiliation with the AAPL. He considered himself to be a "professional policeman' who could care less about Black issues. An upfront statement such as his was generally an early warning that the guy was trying to establish that he had no psychological hang-ups and, in fact, the inference was that he was prepared to forgive me for my Blackness and any hang-ups that I may have, providing of course that I conduct myself in a professional manner. Officer Joe quickly buttressed his position by placing himself in the driver's seat of our assigned patrol car. Customarily, when two officers worked together for the first time, one would automatically ask the other his preference for driving. Generally speaking, Department protocol gives the senior officer great resposibility for the team's activity and overall conduct, including presevation of the vehicle. So this overt actions of "inferred priviledged authority" by Officer Joe did not go unnoticed.

This was to be a most interesting tour of duty for patrol car #1105, whose assigned area was in the heart of the Black community. The first radio assignment we received was a call of "a woman with a gun." Officer Joe turned on all of the vehicle emergency lights and the siren. He drove through several stop signals to travel a distance of six blocks. At one point, our calibrated speedomenter reached 48 miles an hour on residential streets. I looked at this officer as he swerved from one road position to the other. He had the look of a person about to receive his high school diploma. His wide-eyed fixed expression cautioned me to hold my concern about his rate of speed until I was certain that I would not be aggraving an already hazardous situation.

Upon arriving at the scene , we were unable to locate the perpetrator. This type of call very often turns out to be unfounded. After notifying the radio dispatcher that no person could be found and concluding that Joe appeared to be back to "normal," I asked him why he had driven like a damn fool. His reply was "If we could have caught that broad, that wouild have been one less gun on the street for these criminals to use against the police." I was tempted to return my confused "professional" partner back to the police station for safe-keeping. My experience said don't be too hasty.

About 4:00 a.m., we received a call of "a man shot in the alley." This time with virtually no traffic, Officer Joe proceeded to the scene at an unbelievably slow rate of speed. I couldn't help but ask for an explanation as he nonchalantly crept along at less than 25 miles an hour. Joe's response was "Why hurry? They said the guy was already shot." As fate would have it, the call was bonafide. The victim had been loading luggage into the trunk of his car. He was preparing to drive his family to Memphis for a funeral. He had been accosted by a thug and shot three times. He was then rushed to the hospital by ambulance before we arrived. Witnesses furnished that much information, but not much more.

Fortunately, the victim didn't die. We broadcasted a sketchy description of the offender and patrolled the immediate area to no availl. Upon reflecrion, I couldn't help but feel somewhat useless toward our role in this assignment. My partner's previous hurry to "get the guns off the street" philosophy had taken a back seat to his attitude of "the victim is already shot, why hurry?"

This young man was a victim of poor training as well as a few other obvious deficiencies including a nonchalant attitude about the people he was serving. However, I held out until our final assignment of the shift , which came at approximately 5:45 a.m. It was a domestic disturbance. Mr. John Q. had just returned home from the night before and had fallen asleep, fully dressed on the couch. Mrs. John Q, who was known as a frequent caller, wanted her husband taken to jail <u>immediately.</u> Needless to say, we had no intention of removing this harmless, but thoroughly inebriated, man from the safe confines of his home only to waste several man hours of police and court time to address a problem that was so far beyond our scope of capability to resolve.

For some reason, my partner decided to admonish Mrs. John Q. (who was twice his age) for having called the police for such a "trivial " matter. The conversations escalated. Their verbal altercation was about to become a physical one. Before I realized it, I had grabbed my partner by the arm and pointed him out of the apartment. After a heated argument on the way back to the squad car, it was obvious that we would not be able to complete this tour of duty together that night.

Just as we were about to get into the car, a young boy 15 or 16 years-old passed by, pushing a shopping cart, loaded with neatly rolled newspapers. Officer Joe, who was now totally frustrated with me for interfering with his display of "professionalism" with Mrs. John Q., shouted at the youngster, "Hey you, get over here!" The kid (appearing to be as confused as I had felt earlier) responded by walking to my side of the car. Joe then shouted, "What are you doing out here?" The sun was slightly visible in the background. "Delivering my papers," the youth replied. "Just make sure that's all you do, Punk," Joe said. With that Joe started the car and drove toward the police station. When we got into the station, I went straight to the commander's office.

After relating to the commander as accurately as possible the accounts of the evening with Officer Joe, I indicated thatI felt Joe needed sensitivity training. His attitude had been dangerous for himself as well as for me and the people of the community. I recounted Joe's response to my question of why he had taken his frustration out on the kid. "That's why I carry two big guns to back up what I say.". The reaction from this watch Commander was even more astounding. "Officer," he said to me "It's not your job to evaluate your partner. Who the hell do you think you are? Your partner was doing good police work. What were you doing?" he scowled. That commander has since retired, but Officer "Professional" Joe is still working. The irony is that he is now a supervisor. This incident not only demonstrated the ineptness on the part of upper management, it also pointed up how a negative five percent of a system has been able to perpetuate police abuse and a poor oftimes antagonistic relationship between the police and the community.

I am grateful for my military training prior to becoming a policeman. The experience with Officer Joe caused me to rely on my Army background. This para-military institution's policies and practices is a do………..ubled edged sword. It's discretionary power can cut you for trying to correct improper actions and it can reward you for continuing to do things improperly while retarding the chances for real reform.

The white officer that worked with me on the North Side and become what I considered to be a friend for life, wanted to come with me to work as partners on the West Side. He candidly reminded me that we had been working together for almost two years.In his mind, we had learned a lot together and we might as well stay together and continue to learn together. My response was, " I don't think so." I found myself trying my best to discourage any thoughts of us becoming a permanent team. Not actually knowing exactly why, my gut instinct said it was not a good idea. I said stuff like "You know your temper is bad.

I know you're not a racist kind of guy, but your actions would be perceived differently in my community than they are here." Little did either of us know how much of the tale of two cities we were both being prepared to play individual roles with simular goals, the rules of game were yet to be realized. The hardest part of the journeys was just beginning.

CHAPTER 6

FORMING THE AAPL

I was totally disgruntled by the time of Dr. Martin Luther King's assassination, the assination of Robert F. Kennedy occurred later, and finally the Democratic National Convention occurred.) the rest_ The Dr. King assasination and the 1968 Democratic National Convention held in Chicago. I was eager to leave the Police Department and join any group whose objective was raising the bar of community conscousness to get involved and take responsibility for self help.

In April of 1968, I caught a portion of news broadcast about a group of Black police officers announcing that they had formed an organization called the Afro-American Patolmen's League(AAPL). It took a few days for me to locate the people involved in that TV interview. I had been on the department almost three years. I had worked in two distinctly divergent parts of the department and two very different neighborhoods of Chicago–one Black and one mixed ethnic Whites. I went looking for the mindset that came across the airways as a breath of fresh air to me. At that time, I needed a job, the pay and benefits of CPD were adequate, but I was convinced that I had chosen the wrong profession. At least that's how I felt. By the time I caught up with these spokespersons, a week or two had passed. I finally got a flyer and attended my very first general meeting in late

April 1968. The initial group that formed the African American Patrolman's League consisted of, Edward (Buzz) Palmer, Curtis Cowsen, Nate Silas, Willie Ware, Frank Lee, and Obaseki Hodari, aka Jack DeBonnett. I sat patiently listening to presenters and from the conveners of the event. I openly expressed my interest in becoming a part of this powerful sounding struggle for justice within the department that I had taken an oath to serve and protect our communities. I was immediately approached by Edward (Buzz) Palmer and asked to attend their upcoming executive meeting. The few individuals in attendance made me feel welcome and each of them ultimately became like a second family to me. I was introduced to a small cadre of very dynamic Black men who were embarking upon an arena of public service that would become an intrical part of my life from that moment on. Those meetings were held in the basement of a three-flat building on South Luella. I believe Buzz Palmer was the landlord. At the same time I was meeting Renault Robinson, Kermit Coleman and others. During that meeting I became a Vice President of Recruiting. I didn't know exactly what that impressive sounding title entailed right then. But it only took a few sessions of serious discussion for me to find out. This was a once in a lifetime opportunity for me to join a movement that was positioned to change how the police treated me personally as well as and the community that I lived and worked in. Recruiting new members for this bold effort was a task that I wanted and in some ways, needed to to be committed to . The souls that were in this small gathering and the ones who had spoken out in the larger meeting a few days prior had convinced me to my very core that I was in the right place, with the right people at the right time in my life.

In the beginning stages of organizing the Black police officers in Chicago, certain realities became very obvious to me immediately. For example, I learned that prior to the creation of AAPL, there were other Black groups that had been in existance for a number of years, both locally and nationally, including the Guardians of Chicago. Most of these groups were well known in their respective communities as well as to the police department that employed them. Their purposes for existing varied from city to city. Many of them realized the historical racial discrimination against them as officers and as members of their families and communities. There are limited records on how this problem was being addressed from one city to the next, but seemingly, there was no record of any organized concerted effort to address this problem prior to the late 1960's.

In Chicago specifically the unwritten rule for promotions, or upward mobility, as it is sometimes called, for Blacks meant you had to be a member of the Guardians to even be considered by the power brokers who controlled that process. Most of their members who had rank above patrol officer appeared to be seasoned veterans. They had to knOw their job inside and out as professionals. The system, as racist as it was, andcontinues to be, never promoted a Black to commander who didn't have the intellect, experience, and every basic qualification to be a boss. That requirement did not necessarily hold true of their White counterparts. I personally had a lot of respect for the Guardians, but it didn't take long for me to realize that they weren't going to openly challenge the system, as we had chosen to do. They were committed to absolute loyalty, to the police hierachy, right or wrong. Some of us held dual membership off and on over the years. Periodic collaboration between the associations became possible from time to time, but I had no strong long term association with them.

The personalities of the members and leadership that made up this group ranged from down right to the bone, ghetto loving brothers from the hood to the more conservative middle class attitudes, depending on the temperature in the meeting room or the of heat that one might feel from the police department hierarchy. The meetings surrounding the activities that came with the respnsibilies for this newly formed group, became almost nightly gatherings for most of the inner servants of the AAPL.

Most decision makers of AAPL were either enrolled in college or had acquired degrees of higher learning in academic studies. The professionals, who helped with the League's work, too many to ever try to mention in a single document such as this, that served as mentors, advisors and strategist were an awesome addition to our overall effort. The historical collection maintained at The Chicago History Mseum, formerly The Chicago Historical Society, is the true accounting of the many dedicated helpers that rose to the occasion when time and expertise was sorely needed. In the meantime, the learning curve in this environment was huge for me. As a police officer, I had barely finished high school, and the only other schooling I had was achieved while I was in the U.S. Military. I was priviledged to be at the table with people who were focused and determined. I later took advantage of opportunities to acquire more education. My will to fight injustices within the system as an individual had just about gone from me. I saw no logical way to continue to fight effectively in an uphill battle for justice. This painful quest for Justice was heavy on my mind because I had family and friends who had already been caught up in the criminal justice system while they were very young. Additionally, I felt that in many ways, I had missed the civil rights movement. I knew that many people my age, had gone to college, following the American dream and found themselves involved in trying to help the struggle for Black America. Now I was being given a second opportunity to dosomething, to give some of my time and energy to a cause that I had not even completely understood. I had taken so much for granted. I had never imagined not being able to sit anywhere I could afford to sit, especially at lunch counters.

As vice president in charge of recruiting, I thought the assignment would be a cake walk for an eager volunteer like me. After a few non-scientific surveys, we began recruiting in different police stations. We took teams of five to ten off duty members to every district station where Blacks worked.

We were requesting them to sign pledges saying that they would join the organizations if they had an opportunity to do so. The conversations and interactions amongst Black officers during these visits set in motion a source of energy that built a strong Black police organization that opened lines of communication with our community organizations, including the Black churches and mosques. The community began to challenge government at the city, county and state levels to take stronger positions concerning civil rights law violations by the police against Black citizens , as well as focusing on hiring practices that discriminated against Black applicants for local and state police jobs. This opened dialog that provided the foundation for organizing and connecting around the country. The African American community heard and responded to a voice of reason coming from Black officers who worked in urban cities that had been experiencing uncontrolled police misconduct including, physical brutality and the use of deadly force for decades.

CHAPTER 7

BREAKING THE CODE

Generally, most Black officers and some whites privately respected what we were doing, but they publicly shied away for fear of being classified and then possibly crucified.

Suddenly, almost overnight, the subject of "the role of police in a free society" was on the front burner of public issues. The League welcomed the sudden emergence of public awareness as an opportunity to align ourselves as an organization to every single entity that expressed an interest in the police problem, including those with specific responsibilities in the area of criminal justice. We began to write, call, and visit the offices, homes and business establishments in the greater Chicago area. We communicated with legislators, judges, defense attorneys, and a range of private citizens. Discussions began to take on a much broader perspective. We were not just discussing brutality, a topic that had been mostly confined to the Black experience; nor were we discussing discrimination, which was regarded as a Black, Hispanic, and female problem. Brutality, discrimination, and corruption had quickly taken the form of a struggle for justice on behalf of the entire community.

The struggle had begun to address serious deficiencies in the entire criminal justice system. This included criminal justice procedures, the police and the judicial process, police and corrections, police powers, as well as the need to define the role of police in modern society. We found ourselves having to approach the subject from the position of an advocate for change. The League had declared itself as such. It took the forefront in Chicago as the open enemy of injustice perpetrated by fellow officers sworn to uphold the law. This posture rendered us as untrustworthy defectors in the eyes of our superiors and many of our peers. Only time would determine whether or not this approach would in any way impact the areas delineated in our objectives.

Initially, our efforts were characterized by our critics as "bucking the system," "trying to beat City Hall," "making waves," and "You guys are fighting a losing battle." All of these expressions indicated an attitude of defeatism. Each connotes that one should comply rather than resist when the odds appear to be greater on the opposing side. The truth of the matter was that the opposition was not so big, but its ability to exert influence and power was awesome. For example, suppose we hypothetically agreed that there were three components that made up the Chicago Police Department. Next we'll weigh the three components individually and assign each its place on a three part pole, which sums up to 100 %. Let's say that one end of our imaginary pole equals 5 % of the personnel, regardless of rank or race. This group commits criminal acts. They brutalize and maim without justification, and they basically have little or no respect for the law or citizens' rights. This is the negative end of our pole.

Then let's visualize on the opposite end of our pole, the second part that also equals 5 %. The component comprises an extremely honest and dedicated group of officers. This group is the one that would quit the job before they would accept a dishonest dollar; would never with malice or forethought take the life or maim an innocent person. Without hesitation, this group would willingly sacrifice their own lives to protect the life of any citizen. This is the extreme positive end of our pole.

Now let's look at the third (middle) part of this hypothetical pole, the obviously greater of the three parts. This center piece constitutes 90 % and dominates the pole, representing the vast majority of the police officers of all ranks. Their common characteristic is that they are just ordinary people, neither heroic nor dastardly, just folks trying to earn a decent living, raise a family and live a long and healthy life. They just happen to have chosen the profession of law enforcement.

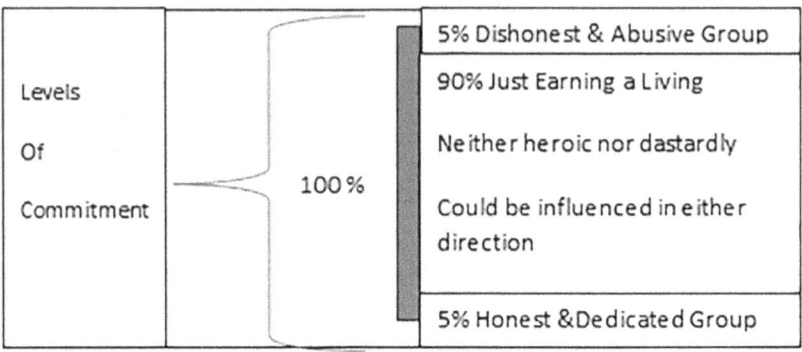

We came up with some answers to the concern of "Why buck the system?" Only 5% are a threat to the integrity of the Department. But the problem arises when the middle (90 %) leans or becomes apathetic towards the negative end instead of recognizing the value I positive five percent. This occurs because the five pecent in the negative group have historically been protected by the powers that be. This has allowed the hierarchy to maintain loyalty and unquestioned obedience from the five percent negative group. In fact, many times they were decorated unjustly after falsifying reports and distorting facts about shooting incidences in which they were involved and unlawful arrests they have made. This reaction by the bosses caused the bewildered counterpart (90%) to follow along as obedient intimidated sheep, acting as though nothing improper had taken place. After all, the acts of dishonesty seemed to earn more respect from the bosses than did the actions of the officer who tried to do his job properly. The misfits were held up as examples of successful cops.

We found that fear and apathy can be replaced by enthusiasm and determination when the potential for change or victory is apparent. A victory in the area of self-respect and public confidence outweighed any threat of retaliation. We were encouraging resistance to a group of hypocrites whose conduct appalled the honest sincere officers, desirous of public support in a struggle against crime. Let's examine a bit closer the notion of improving the relationship between White and Black police officers. Let's keep in mind the hypothetical breakdown (5% positive + 5% negative + 90% apathetic), weighing the possibilities for success in this area. Demographically, White officers of the Chicago Police Department generally come from the Northwest and Southwest sides of the city. These areas have historically been viewed as the most segregated communities of this city. The exposure of these individuals to Blacks has been very limited in practically every respect, i.e. housing, employment, social life, business, worship and etc. To expect them as a group to be concerned about the day-to-day problems of the Black community is asking a lot from the individuals who just want to earn a living.

Consider the attitude of an individual in particular when he learns that there are some black officers who have publicly stated that they will break tradition and speak-out against police injustices against citizens, especially Blacks. To most of them, this sounded like the battle cry that was so commonly heard from the civil rights movement. This cry repeatedly placed Blacks and "those commited liberal whites" on the wrong side of police picket lines. To these White officers, it was in their opinion, unforgivable. They did not see how these Black police officers, who should have been grateful to have the job, could now speak-out against a fellow policeman for any reason. Obviously, none of the whites as a group or as individuals had been subjected to the type of indignities that were so common to Black citizens or Black police officers.

At the time the League organized, there existed other police societies and organizations: the Irish-American Police League, the Polish-American Police League, the Italian-American Police League, the Jewish, etc. No one had voiced any objections to their existence. To form a group with such a militant sounding name as the Afro-American Police League; however, created an attitude on the part of police command personnel that would eventually motivate Black officers to join this group in unprecedented numbers. There was a common bond. We found ourselves castigated from any type of comraderie enjoyed by our peers.

While this was predictable for the known members of the League, we had no idea of how far the opposition would go to make sure that not a single black officer was spared the insults and racist resentment displayed openly by supervisors at all levels of the Department toward the League. It was typical for a White supervisor to pull a familiar Black officer aside and whisper, "I know you're not going to jeopardize your career by getting involved with those 'troublemakers?' They won't last long and they will take a lot of good guys like you down the drain with them." The heirarchy was so doggedly determined to squash the League that they started to mistreat and disrespect non-member Black officers indiscriminately. Their hostility caused many of the moderate Black officers to join the League out of frustration. They were being treated as if they were members anyway. Eventually, more than 80% of the approximately 2,400 Black police officers joined the League within the first two years of our existence.

Both White and Black officers were eager to read *Grapevine*, the newsletter published monthly by the AAPL. It was of interest because much of the focus was on problems in the station houses, complaints of brutality, and discriminatory practices by the Department. After a few months of publishing and circulating our position papers, we began to exchange dialogue with White officers who occasionally found themselves sharing a squad car for eight hours or being assigned to a post with a League member. This prompted the League to put together an educational seminar for the purpose of clearing the air about what the League stood for and conversely, what we didn't stand for.

The relationship between White and Black officers was not in the distant past nor was it then considered to be an easy subject to discuss. Our opinion is that relationships were more tender than before. Several new factors have been added to the list of potentially divisive elements: (A) a union that collects dues from all officers but opposes affirmative action programs which addresses past discrimination against minorities; (B) court imposed quotas that favor Black and Hispanic males and females who otherwise would never reach parity in their chosen professions because of past practices; (C) the first Black mayor and Black police chief in the city's history; and finally, (D) more Black police supervisors than ever before.

In 1972, I was voted in as president of the League, while Renault Robinson became the Executive director. It fell on my shoulders to boost the morale of the members because we were constantly facing harrassment. The following letter is one way that I went about this task.

Breaking the *code of silence for a code of ethics* did not happen in short easy steps. Personally, I had to reflect on what was happening in situations. This is how I learned what discrimination really was.

CHAPTER 8

AAPL MEMBERSHIP TAKES A TOLL

> *I was the guy who literally had to meet just about every Black police officer in Chicago because my job with the organization required me to go to local district stations and do recruiting . . . and that's when we began to get in trouble.*

The accomplishments of AAPL came with a price. Although I was unhappy about the discrimination I had witnessed and experienced, my career was on a relatively good path. My efficiency ratings were very high when I met the guys at AAPL, which was later cited in Federal Court. My evaluations were high. I had arrested people, including rapists, robbers and burglars. I had written a lot of tickets, although most of my work had been in the White Community. I must say that I probably locked up more White people during those years than most Black policemen in their whole careers. It was not that I was harrassing people; it was because of the community where I had been assigned. I left the Uniform Division and went into the Task Force. That was an upward step, causing my efficiency ratings to become higher. The bylaws of AAPL stated that members of the board of directors could not take promotional exams because supervisory positions could result in a conflict of interest and be used against the organization. This was enforced until the late 70's. In many ways, the AAPL organization interrupted my career. It was a price I was willing to pay.

I was arrested so many times. I was on trial for commiting battery against a White police officer on the day that Mayor Richard J. Daley died. Most people didn't know that. I was actually going through a jury trial for a confrontation with a White officer. That officer and I signed complaints against each other. The complaint against him never got to the courtroom. Every time my lawyer raised my case, they changed judges. The judge would recluse himself and move it on to another one. Excerpts from the court proceedings are the following, Kermit Coleman as one of the lawyers for me as the defendant:

The hearing of April 29th, The State of Illinois vs. Howard Saffold, took place in the Circuit Court of Cook County, Illinois County Department – Municipal Division, First District, on April 29, 1976. The Honorable John J. Moran presided.

The Assistant State's Attorneys who were present for the prosecution were Dennis Porter and Mary Ellen Ramey.

My Defense Attorney was Attorney Kermit Coleman, and Attorney Lawrence Kennon was also present.

After the Clerk called the case, Judge Moran asked if we were there on a motion to dismiss the complaint.

Mr. Porter explained that we were having a hearing on whether to grant an evidentiary hearing on a motion to discuss the complaint. However Attorney Coleman said that wasn't the only motion and went on to explain that there was also a motion that was made earlier, first before Judge Michael Jordan on December 2, 1975, and then repeated before Judge Robert Meier, and each of those judges recused themselves. He went on to say that on January 17, it went to Judge Howard Miller.

The motion, he explained, had to do with the fact that there were two complaints sworn out and sign the evening of the incident and when the case arrived in a court for the first time, only one complaint had been filed, which Officer Malloy, charging me with battery, signed.

The second complaint, which was not filed, had been properly executed and signed by me, charging Officer Dennis Malloy with battery, and in that regard, Attorney Coleman stated that the other motion before the Court that day, was to address whether or not the complaint signed by me and against Malloy should be filed. However, he also noted that the file, which had been physically attached to the file in the Court, was no longer in evidence and no one seemed to know what happened to it in the interim. Attorney Coleman stated that there was proof that the file had existed based on "references to it through colloquy back and forth along with counsel and judges from time to time, sufficient to prove to anyone's satisfaction that there was in fact such a file." Coleman reiterated that "It's not there now and irrespective of whether it was there, it's not there now." He stated that, "what we'd like is a motion on whether or not that cross complaint is not a counter complaint that has been referred to from time to time, whether that cross complaint must be filed as well as the complaint, which was filed, and we'd like also a hearing on that and to give some testimony with respect to this."

Assistant State's Attorney Porter countered that

"This case is up for a hearing on whether Your Honor is going to grant them an evidentiary hearing on a motion which has previously been denied. With reference to what counsel is saying now, Your Honor, there has never been a charge filed with the Circuit Court of Cook County against Officer Malloy or Howard Saffold as the complainant."

He went on to say,

"This is not the proper time nor the proper place to be bringing in additional charges, Your Honor. Now, of course, your Honor is well aware that Your Honor can, if Your Honor wishes, to allow a person to file a complaint. That's the prerogative of the Court, to allow a citizen to file a complaint with the Circuit Court. But your Honor, the State's Attorney's Office is not going to file a complaint against Officer Malloy, signed by Defendant Howard Saffold, for the reason that there is already a complaint pending against Howard Saffold wherein Officer Malloy is the complainant and, as to that there has been an investigation made by the Chicago Police Department as to what the appropriate charges should be with regard to those two persons.".

He argued that the State's Attorney's Office is not primarily an investigative body and that the complaint before the Court had been investigated by the Chicago Police Department and the State's Attorney's Office had proceeded on that complaint.

He then instructed the Judge "It would not be proper for Your Honor to make any ruling on an alleged incident that arises out of the same incident where there is already a complaint filed where the would-be complainant is now a defendant."

Attorney Coleman countered, first explaining to the Judge that he and Attorney Kennon had, between them, almost eight years of service for the State's Attorney's Office, and that was the first time he had ever heard that such complaints were not proper, and that the State's Attorney's Office did not, in fact, file them. He added,

"I wanted to just mention one thing which the Court may or may not be aware of. Its relevancy is simply to the response of counsel, not to the merits of the case. However, counsel refers to this having been investigated by the Police Department. Your Honor, it is our contention that it is the Police Department, which is at fault in this matter and that through some impropriety, they failed to file the complaint, which I now allege was improperly filed. I simply ask this morning, so that the Court can be well-acquainted with what the circumstances are, to have some oral testimony this morning and then we can find out whether or not the circumstances under which this complaint was refused filing were proper on not."

Noting that he didn't have the complaint because it was missing from the file, Attorney Coleman stated:

"Now, there is no other way for me to get it except to ask the Court to give it to me. I have before me a copy of a transcript before Judge Howard Miller on the 7th day of January in which I go through this whole argument. The motion is made there. There is, in the text of the transcript, indication that he is at the time holding in his hand a complaint that was filed within ten minutes. When I say filed, I should not ...Let me back up a moment. I thought that used to mean in a police station when you put your name on a complaint and the desk policeman took it that it was then processed and you went to court and somehow, magically perhaps, it appeared on the Clerk's records. Well, in this instance, both the complaints under consideration here, the one you have in front of you and the one that I say now has disappeared were filed."

The Judge asked Attorney Coleman if he ever got leave to file. Coleman responded:

"That's what I've been asking in front of at least three other Judges. The only Judge who had this case that I have not asked that of was Judge Welfeld, and we were in a very hairy kind of circumstance over in Traffic Court that day. So I have asked everybody in front of whom this case has come, please hear this matter because I ..."

At that point, the Judge interrupted Attorney Coleman:

"The only thing is, I don't think I have any authority to tell the State's Attorney what actions to bring or what actions not to bring. I think the statute vests them with the authority to determine what cases to bring and what cases not to prosecute. They can file suit and then turn around the next day and nolle it."

Attorney Coleman said he understood, but that didn't stop him from further making his point:

"The point is that though it may well be the State's Attorney's Office which has been remiss and has been improper in its actions. I don't know. But it is either the State's Attorney's Office, the Clerk's Office or it's the Police Department, among those three institutions, one of them has failed to properly process a properly lawfully drafted complaint signed five minutes one way or the other, I don't know. This one may have been signed five minutes before the other but drafted by the same patrol officer within ten minutes of each other, both identical and one shows up in Court and the other doesn't, and it presents a serious problem for us."

The Court once again said that it was a matter for the State's Attorney, and began to say "If they, in their investigation" Again Attorney Coleman interrupted him:

"But the State's Attorney, by his own words, Judge, what he has said, is not – not only has he no intention of filing it, but his office is of the opinion that it would be improper to file it. Now, I quarrel with his reasoning, and we need for some – for a ruling in which to resolve this matter."

The Judge was not persuaded and said he thought the proper form would be a mandamus proceeding or something like that, but he reiterated that he didn't think his Court was the proper place. Attorney Coleman answered that with another plea:

"Will you at least let me do this, Your Honor? I don't think this will take more than five minutes, but I would like to have reduced to writing a sworn statement with respect to how these two files were – these two complaints, at least, were processed on the night of the incident. I was there. I would like to be sworn and have counsel examine me on that, and then I will at least feel more secure about having reduced the circumstances and our demand with regard to whether it ever gets acted on. Certainly, if we don't get an opportunity to get before the Court, it won't."

The Judge continued to say it was irrelevant to anything that was before the Court, stating the only thing he had before him was a complaint. But my attorney wouldn't give up, saying:

"This is a continuing motion, Your Honor. Judge, this motion was made back when this case first came up. The 2nd day of December, I made this motion for the first time and have repeated it in each instance, each Judge saying that for one reason or another he couldn't hear it. It's a hot potato, Judge. This is a political case. It's a case, in my opinion, where it is, you know – people frequently just don't want to make decisions on such things. They would rather stay out of it. However, somebody, at some point, will have to say whether the police department acted improperly or whether the State's Attorney's Office did. Maybe a Court of Appeal. I don't know. But I certainly would like at least …"

Once again, the Judge interrupted Attorney Coleman, denying the motion, although when Attorney Coleman requested to make an offer of proof the Judge said, "Sure you can."

Larry Kennon then stepped up and said,

"I was only going to include that inasmuch as it is an ongoing motion, the Court questions the relevancy, it was relevant at the time because of the fact we are trying to get everything before the Court that happened on a particular night. Therefore, in order to establish whether it in fact happened in order for me to, under oath, interrogate Mr. Coleman, I think it would be proper with respect to the motion and then the Court having fully all of the facts…"

The Judge interrupted Larry Kennon, asking him what authority he, the Judge, would have assuming everything Kennon said was true, and further saying he couldn't order the State's Attorney to bring an action.

The Judge asked again if what they wanted was to make an offer of proof, and Coleman said that would satisfy us. The Assistant State's Attorney, Porter said, "Your Honor is absolutely correct in what you say. You cannot direct the State's Attorney's Office to file a complaint, Your Honor, so this entire proceeding is not proper."

But the Judge said in fairness, we should be allowed to make an offer of proof, and acknowledging that Porter may appeal the decision, he said the Appellate Court may not agree, but that was the way he ruled.

After a brief discussion off the record, Attorney came back and said,

"Your Honor, on the date of the 21st of November, I was present in the Second District Police Station, which is located at 51st and the Dan Ryan. There were many officers, police officers present. Among those who were present were an Officer Howard Saffold, Officer Dennis Malloy, the District Commander, Erskin Moore and as I say, many, many other people."

"At one period of time I had come on another matter, and I was sitting in the commander's office, having a conversation with him about the matter which brought me to the Second District that morning. There were sounds of a scuffle and excitement in the outer area, upon which we all got up and went out and what we saw was that there were a group of people who were holding Officer Saffold, a group of people holding Officer Dennis Malloy and, apparently some altercation had taken place."

"Upon questioning each one, each said that the other had battered him. Officer Saffold said he had been struck first by Officer Malloy. Officer Malloy said he had been struck first by Officer Saffold."

"Now at that time, the commander had drafted a complaint charging Officer Saffold with batter, the one which appears before the Court now. He subsequently, within – I can't say precisely because I didn't time it, certainly within twenty to thirty minutes, he had drafted a second complaint charging Officer Malloy with battery against Officer Saffold."

"Officer Malloy signed the complaint in which he was the complainant, by Officer Robert White, processing such things that morning. The complaint charging Officer Malloy was then brought by the same officer, Officer Robert White and Officer Saffold was asked to sign the complaint charging battery against Malloy."

"Clear case of cross complaints within thirty minutes of each other for an incident in which the officer in charge, the District Commander, did not see the incident, but simply had to rely upon statements by the people, each of whom gave conflicting statements as to who struck the first blow."

"I stood with Officer Saffold and read the complaint. It was handed to me first. I read it and gave it back to him, told him to sign it. He did in fact sign it, handed it back to me. I then handed it to the officer who was processing such things, Officer White."

"We were then given a court date. I think that date was 2 December. Arriving in court that morning before Judge Michael Jordan, we discovered that only the complaint which had been filed by Malloy against Saffold had become part of the court business for that day. The other complaint was not in sight. The Judge did not know anything about it, of course, and questioned about it. One of the clerks said there is such a complaint and pointed to a drawer at the Clerk's table. The drawer was opened and, in fact, the complaint was there. However, it had been brought over attached to a transmittal sheet and had not been given a number and had not been made a part of the daily court call for that day."

"I then at that point made my motion before Judge Jordan for a hearing on the matter of whether or not that cross complaint should be filed. Judge Jordan at that time said that he would not hear it because he wanted to recuse himself because he and I had been on several cases when he was in the Corporation Counsel and other matters and he said though he could be fair he thought it proper for him to withdraw and he did in fact."

"I did not argue with that. He then sent the case over to Judge Meier, I think for the same day, or succeeding day, when Judge Meier said he could not hear it, and it was then sent a few days later to Judge Howard Miller."

"We went before Judge Miller and again, hear the other questions the Court may have on the matter. But to the best of my recollection, what I have described to you is briefly what happened and in law I am not certain at all how it happened, and I have grave doubts about the propriety of it."

At that point, Porter asked to make a statement, and this is what he said,

"Your Honor I believe – I am not positive, Your Honor, but I believe it is the policy of the Chicago Police Department that if a complaint is made charging an officer, I believe you have – in order for that complaint to be filed through the normal procedures, which I believe entail the police department notifying the Clerk of the Circuit Court a complaint has been filed. I don't know the actual mechanical procedures by which a complaint is physically brought to the attention of the clerks, but it's done through the Chicago Police Department, and if an officer is a defendant in a case, I believe that the customary procedure is to have that complaint approved for filing by the Watch Commander and in this case this complaint was approved by the Watch Commander."

Attorney Coleman corrected him and stated it was the District Commander, and Mr. Porter corrected himself, saying "Alright, the District Commander, in this complaint, in this situation, the District Commander did approve the filing of that complaint. He did not approve the filing of the other complaint."

That was not true, and Attorney Coleman stated it wasn't true. He noted that the District Commander ordered the second complaint at his request and that he went with the District Commander to the place where he met the officer who did the typing, and the District Commander did order the officer to draft the complaint. He repeated what he has said previously, that it was processed up to the point where Saffold signed it and gave it back to the proper police officer, noting he didn't know what happened after that.

Mr. Porter said he had spoken to Commander Moore personally on that came and recalled that Moore told him he allowed the complaint to be typed but he ordered it not to be filed. He expounded on this,

"Inasmuch as Commander Moore is not here, that's what I recall, Your Honor. Further I would like to state that I think Judge Miller's offer to handle this situation as proposed by counsel, I think is the correct situation Your Honor. Inasmuch as we are not primarily an investigative body, and our division, in the First Municipal Division, we have no facilities for investigating complaints, Your Honor, that is done first by the Chicago Police Department. There is a branch in the State's Attorney's Office which does have the means to conduct an investigation, that being the Special Prosecutions Unit. And so it is our policy in the First Municipal District, Your Honor, where a complaint has been lodged against an individual, be the policeman or any other type of individual, that we will not allow a cross complaint to be filed out of the same transaction by a defendant in the case that is currently before the Court wherein that defendant becomes a complainant in the other case for the reasons which I have stated previously, Your Honor. That that places us in the position of prosecuting and representing."

Attorney Coleman said that Porter seemed not to understand that the circumstances are not as he describes them, stating "We are not talking about bringing one later."

Mr. Porter attempted to interrupt Coleman, but the Judge ordered Porter to let Coleman finish, and so Coleman went on to say the following:

"I'm sorry. I wish he would be a little more accurate in what he is saying. Then I wouldn't have to say that. This is not a case where one complaint has been filed and we are trying to file another one. We are talking about contemporaneous complaints and if he doesn't understand that, let me say, that that is the case now because that's what we are talking about. Not filing later, which he keeps referring to."

Porter countered that his understanding was that Commander Moore authorized the filing of the complaint wherein Howard Saffold was the defendant but did not authorize the complaint to be filed where the alleged complaint where Howard Saffold was the complainant.

Objecting to this, Mr. Coleman reminded the Judge that he was an officer of the court, and that Porter was not present, and what he was saying was not true.

The Court asked if hypothetically Commander Moore did authorize it, would it be binding on the State's Attorney's Office.

Coleman said, "I don't know. But let's let the State's Attorney decided who – He admitted a minute ago it was his office. Now he's trying to say, apparently, I guess, that it's the police department that somehow did this through."

Mr. Porter clarified that he was trying to say that he was not going to file a complaint charging Officer Malloy with an offense. And Coleman said, "Fine. I got that message when you first spoke up." He went on to say, "If the Court has any doubts about what happened there, I would ask for a subpoena for District Commander Erskine Moore. We can get him in and I will put him under oath and we'll see what happened.

The Judge repeated that he thought the discretion was not in the Police Department but in the State's Attorney's Office. He sent on to say,

"The State's Attorney is an officer elected by the People, and under the statute they are vested with the discretionary powers of what actions to bring or what not to bring. Or what to prosecute or what not to prosecute. I have to assume they are proceeding in good faith. So what was the nature of your motion?"

Coleman said the motion was for a hearing and for a filing of the complaint charging Dennis Malloy with battery and signed by, as complainant, Howard Saffold, to which the Court responded that the only complaints he had before him were the ones against Howard Saffold. He said "There is allegations of a complaint being filed somewhere, but apparently the Clerk never reached the . . . "

At this point, Coleman interrupted him.

"Not reached. Your Honor but it has in fact, reached the Court. I traveled all the way from the South Side down to Traffic Court."

Porter wanted to "keep the record clear" by stating there has been no allegation that complaint was filed with the Clerk's office, that it was ever docketed on the call.

So once again the Judge denied our motion, saying it would be in the nature of compelling the State's Attorney to file an action, and again he said he didn't think he had the authority or right to do that.

Then Coleman asked the judge for any "additional relief in the matter." If not an order on the State's Attorney's Office, any other order which would accomplish the same effect.

Once again the Judge said he didn't think he had any jurisdiction to do that. "Because the State didn't elect me to be the State's Attorney, they elected Mr. (Bernard) Carey to be the State's Attorney. So then the Judge asked what should be put down, so it would be clearly understood. Motion for direction of State's Attorney to file complaint, denied?

Larry Kennon replied, "No it would be a motion for – Let's say, a motion for Howard Saffold to file a complaint, to be denied."

The Judge said "He's not asking for a complaint today." To which Kennon said, "Yes. What we are doing is asking that the complaint –" The Judge interrupted him, saying "You are not tendering anything."

To that, Coleman said,

"Well, Your Honor, we can't do that because it has disappeared. There was a physical document which constituted that complaint which we never had control over and which only the Clerk's office, the State's Attorney's Office and the Court has had control over."

Porter objected to the mention of the State's Attorney's Office, claiming to have no responsibility for that.

The Judge said he didn't know if it was ever filed.

Larry Kennon suggested that in order to file a complaint, there would not have to be a physical complaint in hand at that time and said if the Court would grant leave of Howard Saffold to file a complaint, they could have him there.

To that the Judge said, "You are not filing the complaint. The State of Illinois files the complaints. He's the complaining witness. Coleman clarified that it was a cross complaint. But Porter said no.

Then Kennon made another suggestion:

"Judge, may I suggest that – we really felt that you would probably let us have the cross complaint and then we would go ahead into this – the actual motion to dismiss the complaint that we – was previously filed. At this point, I would –inasmuch as we do not have this complaint, I would ask for a continuance on this matter and then we'll have a hearing on the motion to dismiss the complaint."

Mr. Porter objected, stating the case had been continued twice and it's not there on a motion to dismiss the complaint, stating:

"Your Honor, the question we are here on is whether Your Honor is going to grant them an evidentiary hearing on a motion which has previously been denied, Your Honor. It's our – and it's our – the motion you just argued."

Larry Kennon, waiting for him to name the motion simply said "Yes?" at which Porter said,

"The file – He know, Your Honor, the motion we were here for an evidentiary hearing on – was a motion which was filed in January of this year. January 16th, Your Honor, to dismiss the complaint, Your Honor. And it is our position, Your Honor that Your Honor should not grant them an evidentiary hearing on a motion to dismiss the complaint, said motion having been denied once already by a Judge of the Circuit Court of Cook County, Judge Jack Welfeld, Your Honor."

The Judge asked Attorney Coleman if in fact the motion had already been denied, and Coleman answered affirmatively, "Before Judge Welfeld, Your Honor." To which the Judge said he didn't think that he had any authority then, and there was no order on that, so it just stands as the previous order.

Mr. Porter then asked that the order read "motion for hearing and motion to dismiss be denied. For evidentiary hearing on motion to dismiss be denied."

Larry Kennon asked the Judge then if they could reopen that motion, to which the Judge replied that there are certain grounds that they can reopen on, if they are properly alleged, adding that he didn't think they could just rehash the same motion, and that he was not an Appellate Judge that could overrule Judge Welfeld.

Coleman then said "Actually, there was no argument on the motion, Judge, at that time."

The Judge asked if Judge Welfeld made a ruling. Coleman said, yes, there was a ruling but no argument.

Porter offered to give the Judge the transcript of Judge Welfeld's proceedings, and Kennon declared that we would accept the Judge's position on that at that time.

Then Kennon said there was also a motion for a bill of particulars. The Judge asked if that motion had been filed and Porter admitted that it was and asked the defense, "We didn't answer that yet?" to which Kennon assured him that they hadn't, and Porter said he would make their answer to the Bill of Particulars prior to the trial date. Coleman said that would be fine, then said,

"At the – the date when the trial date was set for this case it was anticipated by everyone concerned, I think, that we would have all these preliminary matters out of the way much earlier than we have, and the date was set for May 17."

Porter corrected him, "May 14th." Coleman agreed, but added that the May 14th date had become unrealistic. Ms. Ramey complained that they had reserved a whole week for that trial, and Coleman said:

"So did we. And I understand the problems involved, but we are down to a point now where we are not going to be able to get ready for trial by that time because these other matters are just now beginning to be resolved, and we still have the matter of the Bill of Particulars to be resolved, which would be sometime further."

Ms. Ramey said they could physically answer the Bill of Particulars and get it to the Defense the following day.

Once again Ms. Ramey complained to the Court that they had set aside a whole week, and the Judge asked Coleman if he wanted to leave it on that date and see? Coleman said no. The Judge asked him if he knew for sure. Coleman knew for sure. He said,

"I know for sure we won't be ready and we are still talking about two and a half weeks for the State's Attorney's Office to reschedule whatever it is they have to do."

The Judge said, "Suppose you bring these – these people down and it's continued again. You are going to get it worse."

But Coleman was adamant, "I can tell you now we won't be ready and I am trying to avoid inconveniencing both Counsel and the Court."

The Judge then told the Assistant State's Attorneys, "He's trying to give us a date where he reasonably expects to be ready. I can't see where two weeks difference will make that big a difference. June 4th all right?"

Coleman said it was fine with us, the Judge said it was a good date – Friday, June 4, 9:30 a.m.

At that point the hearing was over, and the Court Date was continued until June 4. We went back to court on June 4th and once again the Court Date was continued.

I finally got my jury trial on December 20, 1976. That trial was full of objections and interruptions. One significant interruption was when the Judge interrupted to announced that Mayor Richard J. Daley had passed away.

At the end of that trial, the jury of 12 men and women found me not guilty.

As my activism was intertwined with my law enforcement career, that was one of many lawsuits and court cases in which I was involved. There were other instances where I was harrassed and took issue with the unfair treatment.

On one occasion I had to call on Commander Sims when a white police lieutenant tried to make an example of me. He blocked a Blacksergeant from putting me in the community relations unit for that district. Instead they put me in a beat car assignment in Fillmore. This was to show Black police officers how the police department felt about officers in the Afro-American Patrolmen's League. His action was to demean me to the extent that my assignment was in one part of the district, and he put a sergeant who was one of his buddies in the car with me. The sergeant was instructed to take me off my post over to another part of the district every day until I wrote a ticket. I wasn't writing tickets on my post because it was four square blocks of side streets. I was making arrests. I was locking up burglars and car thieves, but that wasn't his interest. They gave me a three day suspension over the weekend.

I went to Commander Sims and explained the situation. He called in the lieutenant. Lieutenant Murphy (who was actually the infamous Jon Burge's immediate boss in Area 2 years later) called the Commander by his first name. He said, "George, I gave him an order, and I expect him to keep it. I don't expect you to rescind my order." I was shocked at the exchange between them.

The Commander dismissed him (but he remained in the room). . "Okay," Commander Sims told me. "Give me a few days, Man. I'll get this stuff straightened out. In the meantime, just report to the sergeant." I said, "I don't have a few days. I'm not going to do what he's telling me to do right now. It's demeaning; he's doing it because of my Association and I know it. I'm not going to let him do that." So I took it upon myself to go home. I dismissed myself. That was the wrong way, but I did it.

The commander in turn went to roll call that day, I was told, and said that I had disobeyed a direct order, and if it were wartime, he would've had me shot. Now, he said that at roll call.

So back at the AAPL shop, Father George Clements was one of the key advisors. Also the late Senator Richard Newhouse, Attorneys Kermit Coleman, Eric Graham and other community leaders were monitoring what we were trying to do organizationally. They weighed in on the recent developments. We had a membership meeting at the local tavern around the corner from our newly opened office on Jeffrey Boulevard. The turnout was huge. The subject on the table was the opening issue of the police department versus the Afro-American Patrolmen's League, but specifically the thirty-day suspension for Poor Howard.

They asked Commander Sims to come to the meeting, and he didn't equivocate. He came to the meeting and said essentially what they told me he said at the roll call. He said, "I told Howard I was going to straighten it out, but he didn't have time to wait. He defied my order, and I suspended him for 30 days. I am trying to get him fired." He did that. I received a 30-day suspension, pending separation. I did the thirty days. I lost about a thousand dollars in pay, and that thing was pending on me all the way up until the time we had that lawsuit. It was one of several suspensions, pending separation. The catapulting and serving in position had to do with performance and willingness to step out front there as a representative. A lot of individuals got opportunities to stand for the cause. Some did step out and suffered the consequences, while some others chose not to take those steps.

Another incident of arrest was recorded by McClory (1977):

" Robinson, Saffold, and Cowsen had just visited six police stations with copies of the latest letter to the Law Enforcement Assistant Administration (LEAA)and were finishing their rounds at the 5th District(Kensington) station when Lieutenant Kenneth Alexander, a watch commander, told them to pick up their literature and get out.

'We have every right to be here and we're not leaving,' declared Robinson. 'You men are under arrest,' Alexander said. The menacing crowd moved back a pace, and Robinson and his companions quietly walked to the lockup."

'What now?" said Saffold. "They've still got to find an excuse to justify this arrest. We may not get out of here alive."

As the cell door clanged shut, a Black cop named Frank Triplett who had been standing at the back of the crowd came forward. "If you're arresting these men," he said, "I'm gonna sit in there with them. I wouldn't want any accidents to happen to them in there."

"The four waited in the lockup for two hours while Alexander and his associates tried to figure out the next step. Eventually, someone got word of the arrest to Deputy Chief George Sims downtown, and he immediately called the superintendent. 'For God's sake,' he said, 'get them out of that pressure cooker before this goes any further.'"(McClory, 1977, pp. 96,97)

PHOTO ALBUM

Carol and I celebrated both of our 50th birthdays with dear friends Professor Curtis and Zetta Cowsen. On a Jamaican cruise ship, we were dressed for the Captain's Ball.

POLICE, PRISONS, POLITICS, & POWER I

Left to right: William (Bill) Hampton (older brother of slain Illinois Black Panther Party Chairman, Fred Hampton, Howard Saffold, Former Chicago Alderman Honorable Anna R. Langford (16th) and Edgar L. Gosa , past President ('83-'87) AAPL

Fr. George Clements (Founding Chaplain of the AAPL) H. Saffold, Supt. Leroy Martin, Sr., CPD and Renault A. Robinson, Executive Director, AAPL

Stephen Alexander, PhD, Volunteer Research Scholar for the Positive Anti-Crime Thrust, Inc. (PACT) and program volunteer, Nataleen Coleman, Retired Sergeant of Chicago Police Dept. Photo by Bernard Johnson.

Ms. Yvonne Davis, Ms. Gertrude Price and Ms. Wylola Evans were the chief creators/keepers of AAPL complaint files that are now in a collection at the Chicago History Museum. Photo by Bernard Johnson.

POLICE, PRISONS, POLITICS, & POWER I

Former U.S. Attorney General, Ramsey Clark, receiving the AAPL National Law & Social Justice Leadership Award from League President, Howard Saffold (Feb. 1971)

Mayor Harold Washington addressing Black Police and Firefighters at the South Shore Cultural Center (January 15, '87) Left to right: Attorney Thomas N. Todd, Howard Saffold, Renault Robinson and Frank Lee

Members of the Late Mayor Eugene Sawyer's security detail. From left to right, Phillip Pence, (unidentified member), (unidentified member), Sgt. Albert Rowe, Mayor Eugene Sawyer, (unidentified member), Michael Ceja, Howard Saffold, Frank Lee.

Candidate Harold Washington being introduced to a group of Black police officers by Howard Saffold (mayoral campaign) (1982) Photo by Antonio Dickey.

CHAPTER 9

BLOWING THE WHISTLE

In the early 1970's, two members of the Board of Directors of the Afro-American Police League went on record for being interviewed on television by one of Chicago's veteran reporters, Mr. Russ Ewing.

He had learned that some of Chicago's "rogue cops" were using guns and knives that had been confiscated from street activities they were involved in to drop or plant at crime scenes where someone had been shot by the police.

February 23, 1972, the office of the Afro-American Patrolmen's League was contacted by Russ Ewing, a reporter from a local TV Station (NBC). His request was for an interview with anyone from the organization who would share information about a term that was being used called "drop guns," as related to members of the Chicago Police Department.

It was decided by League leadership that myself and Officer William Bigby would consent to that scheduled interview. The interview took place in a section of our office, 7126 South Jeffrey Boulevard. During that time, several police related shootings had taken place in the city. Because we had not agreed to discuss any specific case, we intended to share general knowledge of what the term mean to us, based on its use in the police circles we were familiar with.

Both Bigby and I had worked in the predominately Black areas on the west and south sides of the city. Our strategy included not identifying ourselves beyond the fact of being active members of AAPL and we spoke as representatives trying to help the public better understand the meaning and actions related to the term and why it was being used.

After the program aired, the hierarchy of the Chicago Police Department set in motion an immediate effort to find these officers who dared to discuss police practices without having first received approval from their superiors.

We anticipated some sort of flak from the department. After all, our role was to bring transparency to the public concerning police accountability for actions of this nature.

It took the department into an investigative mode amongst the Black bosses initially. We learned that the superintendents had called a special session for the small group to view the news footage to see who could identify who the voices belonged to. After a few broadcasts, the suspects were narrowed down to two of the League's directors. Almost three weeks passed before an investigative reporter, Walter Jacobson, learned that the police department had conducted an official internal affairs hearing where Officer William Bigby and I had been subjected to an intense interrogation conducted by a panel made up of department superintendents, two lieutenants and a Black and white team of investigators from the Internal Affairs Division. This panel attempted to coerce Bigby and me to participate in their contrived method of punishing our members for speaking out publicly. By 1972, we had learned a little more about how to bring our lawyers into these types of hearings.

The sequent of events went like this:

Bigby and I were assigned to a newly created unit called the vertical patrol unit at the time of the interview. It was called the vertical patrol unit because we were supposed to be serving the residents in the high rise public housing units located in the heart of Chicago's near north side. Ben Austin has written a book entitled "High Rises" that gives comprehensive details on the subject of public housing in Chicago. This housing complex was in a police district that served the downtown business district along with some of Chicago's richest residents as well as several thousands of Chicago's low income families, stacked into a densely populated environment that had become a tale of two very diverse groups of people. Their experiences with police services ranged from the best service and protection that anyone could have received all the way to the poorest possible service or no police service at all.

My story of these two events, one points to how the internal investigation tool was used to discourage us from going to the press, the media and this interrogation by the CPD trying to silence the voice of an organization that had become a daily challenge to their traditional operations. The steps taken by the police department are shown here to indicate the time, personnel and resources this police agency is willing to invest in getting rid of the messenger rather than give the same energy to revealing the problem that the messenger sent.

Here's what was being quoted on April 26, 1972 in the IAD report. Supposedly Sargent Bonner (IAD) had contacted reporter Russ Ewing of NBC and Ewing refused to identify the two officers he had interviewed February 23rd. The report goes on to say that they learned from the commentary of Walter Jacobson a person named Phillip Brail, 4745 South Kimbark Avenue, had written a letter on March 12, 1972.

The plot thickens. Being told no by Mr. Ewing. The IAD investigation accurately used the TV commentary that publicized the name, address and complaints expressed by the author of the letter to construct their line of questions for Bigby and me. They used these two media events to violate our First Amendment rights to speak openly about wrong doing by a governmental agency.

The long and short of this story is the police department challenged us administratively and we refused to participate in this illegal hearing. After excusing us from the room of the hearing, the conveners conducted their hearing without us.

They found us guilty of violating rules of actions and conduct which brought discredit to the department by making statements that were unsupported and participating in a media interview without obtaining permission from our superiors to do so. We both received thirty-day suspensions.

Bigby was to start immediately. Mine was to start upon my return to duty from my annual vacation which I was on at the time the notice came down 22 December, 1972. Before Bigby could complete the total amount of thirty days and before I could start serving my thirty days, an order issued in the form of a memorandum came down from James Conlisk, dated 15 January 1973. This memo was addressed to the three deputy superintendents.

To: The Bureau of Operational Services, the Bureau of Inspectional Services, the Bureau of Administrative Services

From: James B. Conlisk Jr., Superintendent of Police

Subject: Patrolman William C. Bigby Jr., 18th District

The following personnel order is issued concerning the above-cited patrolman:

1. The 30-day Suspension of Patrolman William C. Bigby Jr. Star 11920, effective 22 December 1972, pursuant to personnel order 72-864 is hereby rescinded.

2. The subject is ordered reinstated to active duty as of 22 December and is to be reimbursed for all salaries due and owing as of said date.

3. All inter-department records pertaining to said suspension and the allegations thereto shall be expunged.

The above will be effective as of this date.

Signed by the Superintendent.

Of course, this action cancelled my upcoming suspension as well.

This first story was a harbinger to the outcome of our more comprehensive case in the United States District Court for the Northern District of Illinois, Eastern District, Case #73C2080.

The second story differs in that I share another instance of how we, as members and leaders of AAPL, had to defy certain orders from supervisors due to the immoral nature of the order given to us.

Just before I was transferred out of 047 unit, I was involved in the only shooting of my career.

The vertical patrol unit had been created as a result of two police officers that were slain while walking across an open baseball field almost two years earlier. The office was located on the first floor of a high-rise building at 365 West Oak Street. Both Officer William Bigby and I had been assigned to this newly formed unit supposedly as a result of the 018 (Chicago Ave. District) having not serviced this housing development for nearly two years. We were told that police officers would not respond to calls for routine service. Residents would have to meet the police down at the street level lobby of the high rise.

That's another story.

On the day of my shooting incident, I and another officer whose first name was John, had just finished the 7 am roll call to begin our shift of 7 am to 3 pm.

It was customary for a team of two officers to volunteer to use the only vehicle assigned to the unit to drive up to Chicago Avenue and Larrabee to get doughnuts from the cafeteria at that location. The radio in that vehicle was on the band or frequency of the local police district.

I was riding on the passenger side of the squad car when the dispatcher announced, "a robbery in progress." The address was less than a block from where we were. Neither my partner nor I believed the call to be bonafide. Who would be up robbing in Cabrini at 7 am? Moreover, who the hell would be walking around in the row houses to be robbed, we both wondered out loud. Nevertheless, being that close you had to go and see what was going on if for no other reason than police curiosity, which made us turn down that narrow street called Cambridge Avenue. Just as we pulled in front of that address, the front door of the apartment flew open and two men emerged and both of them took off running in opposite directions. I had seen the one that was closes to me had an M-2 gold-plated carbine rifle with a modified stock. I could also see a banana shaped bullet magazine that would hold at least 15 rounds of ammo. My foot chase was close to a block going in an alleyway that the offender had scaled with me right behind him. As he ran, he would duck behind garbage cans sporadically. Each time he did this, I would stop behind a can also. I was expecting him to engage me in a gunfight each time he stopped because he could only go in one direction. The third time we got back into the open area; I took aim and wounded him in the leg. As I cautiously walked upon him, I ordered him to stretch out his arms so that I could see his hands. I didn't know that he had ditched the weapon behind the last set of cans he had stopped at.

By this time, police cars were coming into the alley from both directions. I yelled, "Hold your fire" as I saw one officer drawing aim at the man on the ground. In that brief moment, as I stood almost directly over him, he uttered, "You tried to kill me." I said, "If I wanted to kill you I could do it now or let someone else shoot you so do not move a muscle." My partner has now driven around to enter the alley as well.

The prisoner was handcuffed and taken to the nearby hospital (Henrotin, I believe). He was given a tetanus shot and sent to the station where I was in the lock up filling out the case report. The Watch Commander came to the place where I was sitting and put down another blank case report and told me to get ready to fill it out because they had captured the other offender. As they were placing him in a cell, I looked up at him and his size and complexion was close to the man that I saw come out of the door at the same time as my suspect. I refused to fill out the other report.

After I finished my report, I left the station and rode back to 365 Oak with my fellow officer. As I found out, just before the shift had ended, that day was payday for several electricians that were working in that housing development and their checks were being cashed inside the apartment the robbers came out of. One of the workers had seen the man who entered the door just seconds in front of him get pulled into the door, which gave him time to get away and run and place the call that we had responded to that morning. A few short weeks later, my Watch Commander, (Lieutenant Nathan Thompson) presented my partner and me a department citation (printed award) in front of everyone at roll call. He then gave me a high sign to come into his office (actually a small converted child's bedroom). We had a mutual respect for each other. He knew that Bigby and I were considered trouble by most of our superiors because of our role with the AAPL.

"Safford, I didn't have anything to do with this." He said as he handed me an official memo that was transferring me to a predominately white district a few miles north of the "Black projects" as Cabrini was referred to by that part of Chicago's near north side.

I knew that this meant another wave of administrative push back from the network of vindictive supervisors. The only retaliation we could pull together in the two days I had before I reported for duty at my new assignment was as follows:

Officer Robert (Bob) Ervin (a member of the board of directors) was also a funeral director in his private off duty life. That day, he dressed in full police uniform. I rode in the back of his family funeral limousine, also dressed in uniform. We drove up to the front of the station at the corner of Halsted and Addison (a busy intersection at 3 o'clock in the afternoon). The front desk was located at this huge picture window. Several police officers were in plain view of us and vice versa. Robert got out of the driver's side, walked around to the rear passenger side, and opened my door as if he was my driver. As I stepped out of the vehicle, he closed the door and we saluted each other and I walked into the station. The look on some of the faces that were about to go into roll call with me was one of the best chuckles we had that whole month. Creative instances like that were a part of the psychological paychecks we received during this journey.

CHAPTER 10

THE DISCRIMINATION LAWSUIT

In short, the League's complaint of discrimination was incontestably valid and a long tedious trial was to take place with the final outcome of this litigation not to be realized until 12 years later. 80 days of trial and 10,000 pages of testimony.

Initially, the lawsuit was being pieced together with a combination of the lawyers who had been working with us, such as Bob Howard from ACLU. Lawyers also came from the Ghetto Project and from other legal groups. We started with limited expectations as to where it would go. I don't think it had been looked upon as a winnable challenge initially. In our meetings, lawyers such as Richard Newhouse, Kermit Coleman, and Eric Graham discussed the merits of the case. The real game changer came when the law firm of Kirkland and Ellis came to the forefront with pro bono help. Much of the documentation of our actions was later published in The Man Who Beat Clout City by Robert MClory.

From my perspective, our biggest concern became the task of identifying victims and preparing people to meet the lawyers, based on what we were alleging. There was a lot to do with the discrimination in hiring portion that was not to come from our members. We were already on the job. Promotions was another body of work for us since we were not taking the exams. Our work as leaders of the League was enough, and we did not need to add more pressure by applying for higher positions ourselves. Assignments—we were not trying to be in specialized units. Our work was to find victims of what we were alleging. The challenge was a combination of mouth-to-mouth or mouth-to-ear exchange. We collected information by socializing in groups, finding former partners, and by collecting war stories we heard in the hangouts. Dozens of different stories were being put together so that the lawyers could begin to strategize and weed out winnable cases.

The lawsuit, in terms of preparation time was several years in the making. I personally remember sitting in endless meetings with the lawyers just sorting through testimonies. We challenged each other with questions like, "How much truth can we prove?" By the time we determined who was actually going to testify from our group, and who could testify in terms of injured parties in other groups, a few of us had become understudies for the leadership team. Renault was the primary liaison between all of the lawyers, including the team from Kirkland and Ellis. Finally, ten people were chosen from our group to testify. I was one of them.

The AAPL officially filed the lawsuit on September 9, 1970 in the Federal District Court of Chicago, charging that its members had been subjected to "unequal treatment, arbitrary suspensions and other harassment" because of their race. In addition to a change in policy, the lawsuit asked for monetary damages. The results of a federal investigation became a matter of record, which was eventually used as part of the findings that proved the City of Chicago was guilty of discrimination in its methods of hiring Blacks, Hispanics and females.

This suit was reinforced in June of 1971 when the AAPL submitted a formal complaint to the Law Enforcement Assistance Administration (LEAA), an agency of the United States Justice Department (CPD). In the complaint, the AAPL charged the Chicago Police Department with purposefully and intentionally using personnel practices and techniques that discriminated against Blacks and other minority groups. The specific charges related to:

> Hiring practices and techniques, including the medical examination of applicants
>
> Methods of promotion to ranks above patrolman
>
> Efficiency ratings
>
> Disciplinary procedures
>
> Assignments within the Department

In response to this complaint, LEAA early in 1972 initiated a study designed to determine the facts in the case and recommend corrective action. One might initially question both the right and the rationale for the federal government to become legally involved in the matter of a local government agency allegedly using discriminatory practices in its employment procedures. There were several reasons for this involvement.

First, both LEAA and CPD were bound by provisions in the fourteenth Amendment of the United States Constitution; second, by the Omnibus Crime Control and Safe Streets Act of 1968: third, by the Civil Rights Act of 1964, Title VI and fourth, by the Code of Federal Regulations.

However, LEAA, in describing the authority by which they were required to respond to this complaint, pointed to the fact that the section of Federal Regulation that prohibited discrimination in employment was not to be construed as requiring any agency or office to adopt a percentage ratio, quota system or other program to achieve racial balance or to eliminate racial imbalance. This fact further indicated the need to pursue a legal remedy through the courts.

The study's findings did become evidence in the litigation of the League's case. Parts of the study revealed that the Black population in the City of Chicago had grown in 1950 from approximately 13.6% (492,000) of the city's population to approximately 33% in 1970 (1,100,000) of the city's population and was constantly increasing.

The team then examined the Chicago Police Department according to its racial composition as of April 1972. The results of the count were an enormous amount of information being aggregated and reported. Part of this information gave a breakdown of police personnel positions and racial count by rank and file.

The information further revealed in part that there were four deputy police superintendents, one Black (25%); 18 deputy chiefs, one Black (6%); 50 directors/commanders, seven Black (14%); 70 captains, one Black (1%); 304 lieutenants, 11 Black (4%); 1,349sergeants, 128 Black(9 %)Investigator, youth officers numbered 1,797, 269 Black (15%); 9,646 policemen, policewomen, matrons, 1,604 Blacks and Hispanics (17%).

In key areas, the hard data showed that Blacks and other minority group members were adversely affected by the present personnel system. The study found that there was a higher rate of serious complaints against Blacks than against non-Black officers. Additionally, it determined that higher percentages of such charges were sustained against Blacks. An even greater disparity was found in the rate at which Blacks were given summary punishment for infractions against Department rules. The study team addressed this problem by recommending among other things the development of a procedure for better control over summary punishment cases by command officers.

The City of Chicago resisted even the recommended administrative remedies advanced by LEAA. The League sued after several attempts to have a judicial hearing were aborted. The League's case was finally assigned to a Federal judge who had been a law professor at the time the case was initiated.

The Discrimination Law Suit was heard in 1975. In February 1976, the memorandum decision and decree handed down found the Chicago Police Department guilty of race and gender discrimination in the selection, employment and promotion of police officers in violation of Title VII of the Civil Rights Act of 1964, as amended.

To remedy the effects of prior discrimination, the court imposed a hiring quota and promotional quota relative to the rank of sergeant. Along with the court imposed promotional quota, the Court also gave the city the opportunity to produce hiring procedures that would not adversely affect minorities. The court told Chicago that the quotas would remain effective until they were no longer necessary. Since then, the City has developed hiring procedures that produce results acceptable to both the court and the Afro-American Police League. The hiring formula was approximately: 30% white male, 30% Black male and 40% was dived between female (20%) Black, white and Hispanic, (10% Hispanic male and other minorities. However, since then the examination process for promotion to sergeant has continued to adversely impact Blacks, Hispanics, and women. A quota remains in effect.

Statistics show that even with court imposed quotas, minority representation within Chicago has not realized any drastic increase in their numbers, contrary to the belief of many so-called victims of reverse discrimination. The most recent statistics show that of 99 exempt personnel (deputy superintendents, deputy chiefs, district commanders, and directors) 24 are Black (25%). Of the 88 captains, one is Black (1.1%); of the 160 lieutenants, 18 are Black (11%); of the 1500 sergeants, 225 are Black (15%) and of the 12,000patrol officers, 2,440 are Black (20%). Hispanics comprise approximately 3% of the personnel, and women account for 7% of the personnel.

The goal of having a representative number of minorities in the Chicago Police Department that will reflect the 1980 census of Blacks, Hispanics, and females will not be accomplished in the immediate future. However, under the Washington administration, the City was on a very positive course of voluntarily maintaining its own affirmative action approach toward a remedy. According to the League's estimate, this will expedite reaching the ultimate goal of equal representation and will most likely demonstrate that the city is committed to balancing the equities in this area and is thereby requesting that white, Black, Hispanic, and female officers share in the necessary sacrifices in order to bring about the change.

With respect to discipline, the court issued a final order granting a permanent injunction and other relief on behalf of the Afro-American Police League. In effect, the order permanently enjoined the City of Chicago, the Chicago Police Department, the Police Review Board, the Superintendent, and all persons and organizations in active concert or participation from engaging in any act or practice that has the purpose or effect of unlawfully infringing on the First Amendment rights of the League and its members. Those rights include, but are not limited to: discharging, suspending, laying off, issuing reprimands or warnings or otherwise disciplining police officers because of their participation in or association with the League or its activities.

Present day League Representatives should have been protected from the atrocities suffered by its founders. The defendants were ordered to expunge the disciplinary actions taken against certain members of the League who testified during the trial and these members were afforded reimbursement for loss of pay due to suspensions, emotional distress, and loss of reputation. This order became law in June 1983. I was one of those League members.

The League interprets this order as a protection for all police officers who choose to exercise their constitutional right to speak out against injustice, regardless of how powerful the violator may be. The impact of these findings is discernible outside the scope of discrimination relative to the Chicago Police Department. The issue of affirmative action is as prominent recently as it was in

1970 mainly because an effective remedy to discrimination has not yet been realized.

From learning the ways of policing as a new recruit to serving to protect during the civil rights era, I can appreciate the laws of the country. We made the impact that we did by exposing discrimination through the law. The African American Patrolman's League is respected around the country because of the victory that was won.

Even though city administrations are still searching for answers, Chicago's success in legally reckoning with the issue of discrimination connected AAPL to other US cities. We helped to form a national organization.

CHAPTER 11

NATIONAL BLACK POLICE ASSOCIATION

You put your best foot forward. You give your best for as long as you can.

The National Black Police Association, originally incorporated in the state of Illinois in 1972, was steadfast in its quest to be useful and accountable to the overall struggle for civil and human rights for Black America.

Initially, that small cadre of thirteen police organizations from around the country convened in a three-day session in St. Louis, Missouri to create a functioning body of Black police officers who would become a voice and a presence for each other, locally and nationally. Our task was to address the issue of how police departments in America were or were not serving and protecting the Black community.

We developed a mission statement, by-laws, goals and objectives that would bind us as a unified group. Our charge was to go back to our respective communities with an enhanced agenda with specific principles on how we were to perform our roles within the local agencies we worked for. This included a firm commitment to be accountable to the communities we lived and worked in.

As I reflect on the span of fifty plus years that are covered in this, my first book, the memory of the many men and women who placed their careers, their actual lives and the well-being of their families in pronounced jeopardy is humbling, to say the least.

These brave souls were just trying to receive fair treatment as they served in this honorable profession. The table stakes were the same for everyone – your life and limbs were on the line.

Some lost their lives or became permanently physically injured in the line of duty. Thousands retired and relocated to quieter communities, and so many of those left the job, suffering with existing medical challenges due to the stress and oppressive conditions they were subjected to in the work place.

Many others of us have been blessed to live a bit longer to continue to network with each other on a level of sharing information that is helpful to those coming behind us in the struggle.

In reflecting further, the active organizers were learning, by way of trial and error, what the real risk factors of our work would entail.

The pushback from the hierarchy and the demands of the community at the street level were coming at us simultaneously.

The significance of the fair housing fight in the cities and the voting rights fight in the southern regions, which were full of real life sacrifices being made by our families, neighbors and friends, was undeniable and shocking.

I mention this part of the risks because of the correlation between voting power and the ability to secure other changes within the criminal justice system. We also realize that if every one of voting age registered and voted consistently, it would not solve the Black problem in America; however, it would be a step in the right direction to achieve our goal of political and economic equity.

Undoubtedly, the work of the AAPL in Chicago was very significant and helpful to the overall struggle we were privileged to be a part of. However, the hardships thrust upon some of the national members clearly demonstrated to all of us that this fight was going to be a long, deep, dangerous journey.

For example, our chapter in Columbus, Georgia consisted of less than a dozen young officers who had just returned from serving in the Vietnam War. They removed the American flag from their uniforms as a symbolic gesture to address the historical mistreatment of Blacks by the police and the refusal of the city to hire more Blacks to be police officers. The leadership was subjected to physical beatings; their family members who held government jobs were coerced into turning their backs on the officers and finally, fired from the police department with a politically contrived out casting that precluded any type of employment in the city, county or state. This happened in the 1970's.

And there was our Chapter in Louisville, Kentucky, headed by the late Shelby Lanier. This man passed on as a result of a severely damaged heart. Shelby had experienced decades of intense struggle with the city of Louisville, Jefferson County and the State of Kentucky.

He organized the few officers who dared to join the Black Organization of Police. During his journey, he ran for public office a few times. Although he never won a seat at the political table, he was not afraid to try. His early information, like every other Chapter in the original NBPA is stored in a digitized collection at the Chicago History Museum's Research Center.

As I segue out of this section of the journey, I must mention the fact that as the new leadership of the National Black Police Association (NBPA) evolved, the group has experienced a separation amongst its directors. There are now two groups.

As I segue out of this section of the journey, I must mention the fact that, the leadership of the National Black Police Association (NBPA) has changed considerably. The original group experienced a separation amongst it's directors. There are now two groups. The newest component created is called the National Association of Black Law Enforcement Officers (NABEO). It should not be confused with the National Organization of Black Law Enforcement Executives (NOBLE). That history is a wholly different story. My mentioning of NABLEO and NBPA is only to say, that as one of the founding elders, I sincerely hope that the true determination and spirit of this powerful movement will never be lost amongst these dedicated public servants.

CHAPTER 12

THE HAROLD WASHINGTON ERA

Mayors Harold Washington & Eugene Sawyers short terms gave us a vision of what police-community relations could be under the rule of an African American mayor.

Because of my role with AAPL, I took a leave of absence from 1975 and again in 1977. During that time, I ran for alderman of the 7th Ward. That's when our organization was beginning to get exposed to the political realities of our work. We learned which aldermen were supporting our cause. My short but educational aldermanic campaign did not put me in the City Council, but it did help us build a few good political relationships and a more entrenched presence in the City. The community organizing and networking was of tremendous benefit to AAPL and also to me personally. The cutthroat no holds barred campaign tactics were a rude awakening.

We had one Black Congressman at the time, Ralph Metcalfe, who was a very powerful ally to the regular Democratic Party, also became a close ally to AAPL. Congressman Metcalfe spoke out against a well-publicized police abuse incident in which Dr. Herbert Odom, a Southside dentist, was brutalized by the police. The late Mayor Richard J. Daley, after appealing to the Congressman to back away from the public outcry, became so humiliated with this act of rebellion, that he took the full weight of his power and ran a handpicked candidate, Erwin France, against Metcalfe. Daley's action sparked a bitter, retaliatory cord in the Black community with his heavy-handed publicly displayed bossism. Metcalfe defeated his opponent handily. Because we had been managing a serious anti-police brutality program a few years before this incident occurred, the AAPL entered that battle with eager determination to help break the traditional chains that the Democratic Party had maintained, since most of us in our twenties and thirties could remember.

After engaging in that campaign, we landed in the middle of the political arena in Chicago. It was during that time that I met Harold Washington.

The major issue at hand was the infamous Stop and Frisk Bill. The CPD began showing a pattern of behavior that reflected the Terry vs. Ohio conduct. It resulted in out-of-control police abuse of authority in the Black community. We began to approach Black legislators in Springfield; State Representative Harold Washington and State Senator Richard Newhouse were the main point persons who worked to rescind this legislation. Every active group in the Chicago, Cook County, and the State of Illinois were all in the middle of the Civil Rights Movement. That caused so many of our destinies to cross at that time in history. I got to know more about Harold Washington when I volunteered to work with his small three-man security operation that traveled back and forth to Springfield. I was on leave from the Chicago Police Department during time, so the League asked that I help perform that function. The hours were long and the pay was short, but we had to make it work.

After the death of Mayor Richard J. Daley, Michael Bilandic became mayor. When I returned to active police duty, my career and AAPL faced another challenge: Chicago's first female mayor; Jane Byrne assumed the office by defeating Mayor Michael Bilandic. She brought in the police union, the Fraternal Order of Police (FOP), which was the beginning of our economic demise. Our first real hit came because 80 percent of our annual budget came from our membership dues. The first FOP contract had an agreement that ended payroll deductions for everyone except the sole bargaining agent. We took the hit as did all of the other groups. Since it was happening to all of the organizations, we could not cry over that. It also impacted our organization in another specific way. It started the unionization of police services in such a way that collective bargaining eliminated the public input. In other words, there was no aldermanic pressure that was being applied to police services because the collective bargaining was an agreement between the City Administration and a group of police officers.

They started enacting basic ground rules for how the police were going to be conducting their business, limiting the disciplinary process that a citizen could use for redress. It compelled us to rachet up our already existing Police Brutality Complaint Program. We had been documenting misconduct as far back as 1970, but we had not before related it to unions.

Jane Byrne's decision to appoint her two top security team members to exempt ranked Police Personnel, gave them the equivalent rank to that of commanders of police. Her decision set a precedent. Subsequent mayors have that same executive privilege going forward. As fate would have it, the first Black individual won that seat in 1983. He appointed me to the position of chief of security, and with that appointment, I automatically became the first Black chief of security in the history of Chicago. This assignment meant that I had to come off my authorized leave of absence from CPD to assume this role to protect our first chief executive. Harold Washington had been sworn in as the public servant who would go down in history as the mayor for all of Chicago. His agenda created new policies and new hope for the people of the city.

My new assignment adversely affected the leadership of our parent organization immediately. The first interruption occurred when Renault Robinson, who had become the primary leader and spokesperson for AAPL, accepted an appointment from the then Mayor Jane Byrne to the Chicago Housing Authority Board of directors. Duties and responsibilities had to be shifted locally and nationally. The challenges for the type of organization we had put in place brought demands on us as advocates that we were not totally prepared for. As police officers, with families to support, we had willfully taken a position against a system that we depended upon for our livelihood. On the other hand, the community that we cared about had no idea what internal pressures for us would be like. We didn't either. To the average person in the Black community, we were viewed as men and women who should stand up for justice. Our complaint program became the primary image of real police accountability. The kind of overt resistance to our organization from the city administration and the Chicago Police Department literally shocked the people of the community. It wasn't long before we felt the direct impact of that shock in a well-entrenched, well-structured way. The challenges for the AAPL on the local level had now shifted to the national arena. The National Black Police Association that had been organized in 1972 was experiencing escalating police community relations problems all over urban America. At the same time, our communities were electing Black mayors for the first time and fighting to retain others that were already in office. Cities like Gary, Detroit, Atlanta, New Orleans, Cleveland, Los Angeles and Compton, were a refreshing reality for people in the struggle for a better life for themselves and their families.

Accepting the task of Mayor Washington's security detail required me to relinquish my day-to-day responsibilities with the organization, locally and nationally. The second level of our leadership, from the office of president all the way to the directors, had been caught in a totally demanding and in many ways, unfamiliar transitional type of restructuring of our community-based operation. The new assignments took a tremendous toll on certain key organizers who had already paid dues of great personal sacrifices as volunteers in positions of service that sometimes didn't even render a verbal "Thank You" to them. However, these individuals were truly a rare band of souls that had tremendous commitments to each other and to each other's families. We had taken an oath to become police officers. As far as we were concerned, the adverse impact on our ability to continue our work in the areas of police accountability, and total police reform came with the badge. That charge was and is a part of our local and national commitment to the community that produced us.

This new responsibility for me was met with a degree of ambivalence. I loved the fact that we were helping to bring about social change. The mayoral appointment had catapulted me from patrolman to the rank equivalent to a Commander, because of the responsibility of this specialized unit of the police department.

It required critical training that had to be learned and put into practice, literally on the fly. As sworn officers, we all had been trained to do routine police work. However, executive protection was all very new to me and the men and women that I was responsible for. The formal training was very helpful and necessary, but the day-to-day lessons that came with the job of protecting the first Black mayor of Chicago had not been written in anybody's book. That experience came by way of trial and error and a double dose of hard knocks. However, this book does not contain the details of that story. This work is more about breaking a code of silence based on a code of ethics. Becoming the head of Mayor Harold Washington's security detail gave me an opportunity to see policing from a holistic perspective that comes only once in a lifetime for a most unlikely guy like me. A peek inside of the room where the command level decision makers sit afforded me the opportunity to see the other side of what we were up against for the last several decades. I was now an exempt person. I actually attended exempt personnel meetings. The resentment was obvious. But the pushback was limited to mean looks only. The mayor had approved my request to add that to my function initially. I knew it was temporary, but we both agreed on the need to establish an understanding of what my presence meant politically. Eventually I disappeared from the early morning meetings as suddenly as I had appeared. One of the first things that I couldn't help but notice was the kind of pressure Black

POLICE, PRISONS, POLITICS, & POWER I

exempt personnel had placed on them. Especially the district commanders. Most of them were noticeably intimidated by their superiors, 99 percent of whom were white, whose power to get them demoted back to their civil service rank was just a few feet away at that table. They were compelled to sit in ridicule while crime reports relating to their respective districts were thrown in their faces as if they had committed the acts themselves. If anyone of them dared to mention root causes of crime, i.e., lack of employment, lack of education or training, they knew their days at the table would be shortened. There were plenty of examples for them to see. They had all witnessed the musical chair games being played on the Blacks of higher ranks. The most regrettable of this two-sided blessing was the interruption of the sorely needed organizing we had been doing in this part of the criminal justice area. As we began revisiting the role of the police in the Black community as it impacts police-community relations. We had to look more closely at mass incarceration and recidivism patterns from at least a political and an economical perspective.

Let's look at the role of the first Black mayor. How did his election impact the police attitudes and services to the community? The community that produced this man of knowledge and wisdom brought his entire political experience as well as his sixty years of life to the office.

His vision for the City of Chicago was a progressive vision that enabled him to form a diverse cabinet of professional, dedicated men and women who truly had the people of the city's best interest as their first priority. With this team of public servants at his disposal, they collectively designed and proudly left in place after his death, a blue print, that if followed properly and fairly could help Chicago to maintain the status of a world-class city for generations to come.

The resistance to the mayor's progressive platform is now commonly referred to as "Council Wars."

Harold Washington was a master of strategy. One of his tactics was from time to time, to take one of the 29 aldermanic opposers with him on his tour of their wards. He would ask the constituents, "Do you want better paved streets? Do you want your garbage removed in a timely way?" They would answer "Yes," Then he would point to their alderman and say, "Tell him to work with me on these types of matters."

The Washington Administration embraced Affirmative Action, but due to the historical nepotism, it was still problematic. As relates to the Chicago Police Department, a frequently asked question was fair: "Does the Department share leadership jobs fairly, with all of its members?" Well, it was common knowledge within the ranks of the entire sworn members and the civilian employees that those slots were being passed from one generation to the next in the same families. The irony of the whole matter came to the forefront when the AAPL lawsuit finally went to trial in 1980. Prior to our lawsuit, all of the white ethnic police organizations in Chicago were all saying the same thing, "The Irish got all the best jobs." "Us Italians got nothing" "We Polish don't get our fair share; we don't have no bosses."

The Leagues historical response was, "Why don't you guys raise hell about your members and stop acting like our organization is doing something wrong?" Our initial reason for forming in the first place had more to do with the mistreatment of our community members including a double standard of discipline toward Black police officers. The discrimination in hiring, promotions, and assignments came second. These core issues became an ongoing discussion and a critical bone of contention to this very day.

Working as head of security in the Washington administration has given me a perspective on politics in general and local politics in particular. Politics in Chicago has its own uniqueness, but in many ways, it is also a microcosm of Politics in America. Politics in Chicago or in America can become a strange animal when in the hands of unsavory people. The complexity of issues came with what I call "the challenge of CERN, my created acronym for Corruption, Excessive force, Racism and Nepotism.

November 25, 1987 was a sad day in history for all who had come to know Mayor Harold Washington. I had been on duty late the night before and was in route to City Hall to start another of my routinely long days when I received a radio call from shift team leader, Frank. I immediately went to Northwestern University Hospital, instead. When I got there, the mayor was still alive, and a few of us were allowed in the room while they were working on him. At that point, we were still hoping for the best, but there are a lot of things that go through your mind. I did not get to exchange final words with him because he was in a comatose state.

The hour of hope had passed, and we had to accept the fact that Mayor Harold Washington was dead. I had a numbing feeling for a long time because I knew what had been interrupted. I mourned for the loss of things that had been put in place but not materialized. Harold knew that his tenure was not forever, but he thought and planned as though he would be in office for at least 20 years. My mind went to who was going to continue this fight. Personally, you were losing a good friend…spiritually, you don't forget him. You can never get prepared for what was going to happen. That morning was a bleak point in my own existence.

The mayor's press secretary, Alton Miller gave more details about the events of that morning:

"In addition to the medical team working on the mayor's body, Howard Saffold, Health Commissioner Dr. Lonnie Edwards, and the Health Department's Dr. Linda Murray were standing in the room. Linda and Lonnie translated for Howard and me as the hospital's new, state-of-the-art heart-lung machine that was connected and procedures attempted. But I didn't need any translation; I knew that if there were a chance of saving the mayor's life, none of us, in our non-sterile street clothes, would have been in the room. "(Miller, 1989, p 13).

Earlier on that morning, it was reported that the Mayor ate a light breakfast. He went to a Southside housing site dedication before going to his office. Miller had noticed that he did not have his usual type of energy. The Mayor asked for cough drops, which were given to him.

The staff was used to having him take a 15- minute nap in the limousine and rebounding with vigor. The press secretary reported that they went to their duties at City Hall. He was in the office with the mayor and noticed that he had gasped and slumped over his desk. Miller quickly got emergency assistance and rushed him to the hospital (Miller, pp.2-9).

The mayor was pronounced dead by the medical staff of the emergency room without ever gaining conscientiousness. The political haggling both publicly and behind the scenes could not have been more destructive to the communities he had loved to serve, especially the African American community. The role of the security detail was pivotal between Mayor Washington's immediate family members, the Chicago government officials, certain community organizations, and his immediate staff and cabinet members. Our input was solicited from all of the stakeholders who thought we could be of help in the immediate preparation for his funeral. Aside from the internal jockeying for protocol positions on the government side, the political pecking order of who was going to be performing the various functions, to say the least, was not unnoticed by me and the mayor's younger brother, Ramon. Our friendship had been developing from earlier years because of our mutual appreciation for the struggle of our community in Chicago with all of its undisputed historical racism and discrimination. His only request to me was that we remain in constant contact until the funeral was completed and that we treat the family with the dignity and respect that they so readily deserved. In retrospect, I am deeply saddened to report that the final home going for Chicago's first Black chief executive, in reality, was the last time true unity between the City elected officials and its residents had been observed by anyone. The mayor's dedicated and most trusted personal secretary Delores Woods was working closely with the other family members who were not local as well as was the Mayor's fiancée, Mary Ella Smith.

The mayor's pastor, Rev. B. Herbert Martin chose words for the eulogy that certainly summed up the greatness of Harold Washington.

At the end of the viewings, the sayings, and the beautiful songs, the security detail guarded the mayor for the last time. Alton Miller put into words what many saw and felt:

"The coffin bearing Harold Washington's body, after having been carried into the church by high-ranking police brass, was carried out by the men who had guarded the mayor. Now, I have no idea what it is like to carry a man's body on his final journey after guarding it around the clock for almost five years. However, I imagine it is something like the crazy kinship reporters feel for the people they cover, through good news and bad news, only multiplied many times. The men carrying Harold Washington's body were strong men, but at that moment even those in the television viewing audience could see they were not devoid of tears." (Miller, 1989, *Chicago, Il.*)

There were some of us that knew the aftermath was going to be much more of a challenge than most people realized.

The first unpleasant task after the mayor's death was to dispel the many theories that some people had formulated about the cause of his death. Some outspoken activists were in rumor circles as well as public media, announcing that Harold Washington was murdered. They had no proof of their charges, yet they convinced many to believe these accusations. This caused a problem for security because some thought we had not protected him enough. It was a problem for the mayor's staff because some of them became victims of unwarranted rumors laced with suspicion.

At the very beginning of the first term of office, he and I actually wore the same shirt size. We found that while on an out-of-town trip one of his aides asked me what size shirt I wore. The mayor had soiled the only white shirt he packed for the trip and had used his spare for an add-on event. I was the closest to his neck size. That fact changed before any of us working the day-to-day schedule even realized what had happened. One day during one of our occasional casual conversations in between outside events, I said to him, "Mr. Mayor, do you know that you have gained more than 20 pounds since you've been in office. His personal secretary, one of the few in-house crews that talked amongst ourselves about such concerns, had thought to install a step-on scale next to the coat closet we all used in her office area. His usual abrupt, defensive response was "You take care of my security, and I'll take care of me." His general attitude, whenever the subject of health came up, was that the fast-paced work of being the mayor of the people of Chicago provided enough exercise. He had convinced himself that there was no need to have a routine exercise program or scheduled physical examinations. His personal primary physician was coercive enough to persuade him to receive occasional sporadic visits. Regrettably, there was never a satisfactory routine that either his security or his personal inner circle could make happen. The city of Chicago was never the same after the death of its first Black Mayor.

Without consulting anyone, I decided that we could not fake our function in the role of security. We were about to receive a fleet of vehicles and keys to doors and offices that I had never seen before. I had police officers whom I trusted with my life, but they were not any more familiar with this new territory than I was.

I got the idea to use a person who had been on the previous mayor's security detail. I thought if I offered him my second in command spot while receiving the same salary as mine, it might work with a limited amount of political fall-out. But that was nowhere near the risk of trying to feel my way forward in complete blindness. I went to seek out one of the Black officers I had observed working security for Jayne Byrne for the length of time we had been campaigning in the primary election. I thought surely, he had to know the operation even though he had not been in charge of it.

I had to depend on my instincts. There was no time to do much more than have a one-on-one conversation with him. My first question to him was, "would you be interested in working for the man who just replaced your previous boss?" He knew the salary better than I did. We agreed to give it a shot for six months. I trusted him enough to gamble on his word.

I told my closest few team members what I was doing. I knew that their reaction would be a good sample of what to expect from the principals who had asked me to accept my assignment. My explanation was simple. It was easier to keep an eye on him than it would be to learn everything I needed to know on the fly.

I was in an on-the-job training mode as far as the operations level was concerned. But there was no room for error at the political level. We were at war. Period!

Immediately we were brought up to speed about the role of formal training available from the FBI instructors on driving techniques, security formations and how to get in and out of the most frequently visited locations in the downtown areas and buildings.

The first time the mayor noticed from the previous administration, he gave me a me a "we gotta talk" look. We had the conversation and I was reminded that the buck would always stop at my door.

Six months passed rather quickly. I had recruited all of my needed manpower to handle a personal detail, house detail and on site City Hall detail.

I had to attend an executive seminar at the FBI academy where several chiefs of smaller police departments were present, to better learn how and when to interact with federal law enforcement agencies and agents.

My assistant, Terry Hilliard, stayed on longer than we both expected, but he eventually went on to further his career, rising to the rank of Superintendent of Police. . My selection for his replacement was one of the founding members of the Afro-American Patrolmen's League.

The overall experience turned out to be a win-win. The mayor did not miss the chance to ask me what took me so long.

November 1987 was approximately 22 months before my retirement age and was a time for many unpredictable events.

The political harrassment appeared at the time of my retirement. The controlling agents tried to block my pension. Because of my years of involvement with AAPL, they were actually blocking my career service time to the extent that my 25 years were null and void. Our lawyers had to go into Federal Court and compare my leave with that of the Police Union head taking leave to work on issues. I did not retire outright. I had to sue for my pension.

After the death of Mayor Washington, I was asked to remain in command of the executive security detail. The request for my retention in the position was twofold. I was retained for the purpose of two necessary transitions. First, the entire security detail including me was to serve a very brief security role to accommodate the turnaround time for interim mayor Alderman David Orr. Alderman Orr personally preferred that most of our routine functions be minimized to accommodate his less demanding lifestyle, as well as the legally required process, that required that the security operation remain intact, up to and during the voting procedures required to select a member to complete the unfinished term of Mayor Washington from within the City Council. The new mayor emerging from the process inherits the same protection as his predecessor and he or she is able to appoint the security chief of the police detail. Both the new mayor and Police Superintendent Leroy Martin Sr., who had been recently appointed by Mayor Washington, asked me to continue to serve primarily in the role of maintaining the already well-trained security detail. The stabilization we brought to the current situation was obvious to both men. My personal respect for both of these men helped me decide to accept the offer, although my acceptance did come with a certain amount of ambivalence.

This community-involved controversy necessitated the in-house election of the city's second Black mayor. The division that occurred had posed an even greater security demand than the one we had encountered with Mayor Washington. Prior to his death, a shifting of power had been moving forward with a new momentum. Now the community energy behind that movement was divided, and the obvious naysayers and political resisters that openly opposed that shifting of power were perplexed about who their enemy was.

Some people, including me, had seen an organized concerted, contrived public campaign to turn a coalition upside down because it had not had time to regroup and cement itself. Its cornerstone had been taken away. As professionals, our role as a security detail was not foggy in any way. The reality of being in the middle of watching the destruction happen did make our job a little more difficult from my perspective. No one could have ever imagined that this type of chaos was even a possibility. In addition to overseeing the team of officers responsible for protecting Mayor Eugene Sawyer's physical safety, our role as a respected part of the community, the day-to-day challenges of following the performance of the late Mayor was not going to be easy for any person, period! To say that Eugene Sawyer's new position in city government was untenable is an understatement. The stability of the entire city was challenged and subsequently its progressive clock was turned back socially, economically and to a great extent, spiritually. The proof is in the pudding.

Some Chicagoans have expressed their opinions, both orally and in writing, concerning the term of service by Mayor Sawyer. Those who choose to pass judgment should be honest enough to admit that no one except that man himself endured that specific challenge. No matter what you say or do, the raw truth is, the rest of us can only speculate as to what we might have done if we had been in Mayor Sawyer's shoes. The late Mayor Eugene Sawyer and I shared a mutual respect for each other. I witnessed his open regret for some of the mean-spirited rejections he received from some members of the community he loved so dearly.

This much I do know – Mayor Washington was not grooming anyone to be his successor. Why would he? His plan for serving the people of Chicago went beyond any immediate future.

I remember the day a 10–12-year-old boy caught us as we were about to pull away from an event. I was in the front passenger seat of the car. Mayor Washington saw the youngster running toward the car at full speed, and he told us, "Let's hold on a minute." Breathing very hard the kid said, "I just wanted to say hi to you Mayor Washington." After a few seconds of complementary words, the mayor told his young admirer, "You just keep getting good grades and I will hold this chair for you." And the youth replied, "That's okay. You keep being the Mayor, I want to be President." With that in the midst of hilarious laughter by us four men in the car, the Mayor waved and we pulled away to head to the next event.

One of the pleasant tasks of my retirement was to present the car that was used by candidate for Mayor, Harold Washington to the DuSable Museum of African American History:

Book I covered more of the Police and Prison of my work.

Book II will lean more deeply into the Politics and Power aspects of this systemic contemporary story (what role does police unions play; political power brokers, community based organizations (CBO's), faith based institutions and lobbyist?

These and other critical topics will be addressed. Thank you for your readership.

POLICE, PRISONS, POLITICS, & POWER I

City of Chicago
Eugene Sawyer, Acting Mayor

Department of Human Services
Judith Walker
Commissioner
Kraft Building, 8th Floor
510 North Peshtigo Court
Chicago, Illinois 60611
(312) 744-4045

August 24, 1988

The Honorable Eugene Sawyer
Mayor, City of Chicago
121 N. LaSalle Street, Room 507
Chicago, Illinois 60602

Dear Mayor Sawyer:

I would like to thank Police Officer Howard Saffold, Coordinator of Security, for the professional services he provided on June 8 of this year at Jenner Elementary School in the Near North Cabrini community.

During the Gang Abatement Workshop Series of that day, Officer Saffold delivered an oral presentation; engaged the students in a group discussion and conducted a questions and answers session that promoted positive communications and interactions among the students. His style of presentation, method and techniques are admirable. The information he presented was timely, comprehensible and applicable to today's times and trends. I am most appreciative to you for sparing him for that time.

Mr. Mayor, the Gang Abatement Program will resume when schools reopen this fall. I would like to ask - if Your Honor would consider allowing Officer Saffold to assist my staff on a "more" regular basis.

Schools in the Chicago areas are in dire need of role models like him, the Cabrini community, specifically. Officer Saffold is indigenous of that community. He projects the confident and successful images needed when working with elementary school youths.

Again, Mr. Mayor, the school as well as my staff would be honored if you could allow Officer Saffold to spend more time assisting them and the students during workshops at schools in the Near North Cabrini Community.

Your consideration is appreciated.

Respectfully,

Robert E. Martin, Director
DHS, Chicago Intervention Network

cc: Judith Walker, Commissioner
     File

HOWARD SAFFOLD

Can you see the drift Brothers?

Again I say, as individuals we are almost helpless. Is this not an obvious indication of how badly we need a strong organization to stand up for our principles as men?

Attorneys Eric Graham and Kermit Coleman are available to defend all active members against these obvious racist tactics, while we strive to improve the relationship between the Police Department as an institution and the Black citizens of this city.

Incidently, you may have read or heard about our request for the firing of Supt. James B. Conlisk, Jr. This was not an act of revenge or retaliation for the unjust suspension of Renault Robinson; in fact, this request is based on very sound inadequacies of the Superintendent and his present administration.

For example:

1. The many unpunished killings of Blacks by white policemen

2. The uncontrollable police brutality and abuses against black citizens

3. The failure of his administration to integrate the Police force as ordered by the previous (1965) administration

4. The failure of the Superintendent to deal with the growing friction between white and black policemen

5. By settling disputes between black and white policemen by arbitrarily ruling in favor of the white policemen

6. The contracting, by Conlisk, of guns confiscated from citizens and presenting of these arms to high ranking Army officials for their own personal use.

7. The Black Panther police investigation which culminated in the Federal Grand Jury report critical of Conlisk and the department, stating that they had made a botched up and bungling job of the investigation.

In view of these shortcomings on the part of Supt. Conlisk and his present administration, we feel that they should be replaced as soon as possible so that citizens of this city might begin to regain some of their lost confidence in the present administration.

Yours in Brotherhood,

Howard Saffold, President

POLICE, PRISONS, POLITICS, & POWER I

Dear Brother:

Black leadership has emerged from among your rank and file. We have been afforded both the opportunity and know how that will enable us to effectively deal with the many problems that we face because of our chosen profession.

This organization after three short years of existence has molded the framework of an image that far surpasses any historical face of black policemen.

No wonder so much opposition is presented to an effort that would remove the obvious double dealing that is practiced by our white counterpart. Today you are saying in a very loud and clear voice, "I'm a black man first." For any individual or group of individuals to not realize our position and responsibility to our people is to say to us, in no uncertain terms, 'that's your problem'. Consider the hypothetical situation if you will, that white people were subjected to the type of abuse and indignities at the hands of any police agency that Blacks are subjected to, I doubt very seriously if they would take the same position that they ask us to take (you're policemen first).

What I'm trying to say to you Brother, is, be very honest with yourself when considering your role and obligation to your community, so as not to betray the trust, and destroy the hope of your people of enjoying the service and protection they need so badly during this time in our history.

In very recent weeks our superior officers have displayed a very open and regretful attitude toward certain Brothers in their time of need and distress, thereby making it more clear how much black policemen need one another.

I bring your attention to these very recent incidents:

1. Officer Lamont Knazze was shot three times by a white policeman without any provocation only to find that a department investigation sought a two (2) day suspension for Knazze for some rule violation. (Justice)

2. Officer Charles Ferguson was shot twice by a white security man on 14th and Homan Avenue only to have aggravated battery charges placed against him, for returning the fire of his assailant. (Justice indeed.)

3. Both Robert Ervin and Ocie Brown were disciplined and degraded by their superiors for interceeding when they saw white policemen using unnecessary force on members of our race. (Rules indicate this is the action to be taken in such cases.)

HOWARD SAFFOLD

OFFICE OF THE
SUPERINTENDENT OF POLICE
CHICAGO

LeRoy Martin, Superintendent

08 March 1991

Dear Officer Saffold:

Permit me to take this opportunity to wish you well on the occasion of your retirement from the Chicago Police Department. We are losing a valued employee, and shall miss the conscientiousness and dedication with which you have performed your duties these past twenty-five years. Your many close friends in the Department will also miss the daily contact they have had with you.

Mixed with this regret, however, is an overwhelming feeling of satisfaction that it gives me when a fellow officer changes direction in life, whether that change involves a new career, travel or just a well deserved rest.

On behalf of the Chicago Police Department and all the citizens of this city, I extend my sincerest thanks for a job well done, and I wish you and your loved ones much happiness in the future.

Sincerely,

LeRoy Martin
Superintendent of Police

Officer Howard Saffold
6700 S. Crandon
Chicago, IL 60649

DEED OF GIFT

TO

THE DU SABLE MUSEUM

OF

AFRICAN AMERICAN HISTORY, INC.

hereafter referred to as the "Owner" of the property described below, hereby gives, transfers, assigns, and delivers all of the Owner's right, title, and interest in and to the property described below, including all copyrights, both common law and statutory, which the Owner may possess in said property, to the Du Sable Museum of African American History as an unrestricted gift.

Dated this __10th__ day of __NOVEMBER__, 19__92__

_____   _____
(Signature of donor)   (Signature of donor)

DESCRIPTION OF PROPERTY:

A four door blue 1982 Oldsmobile Regency originally owned by the late Mayor Harold Washington. This automobile was used by Harold Washington when he was a U.S. Congressman campaigning for the office of Mayor of the city of Chicago in 1983. The automobile is in operational and intact and was legally purchased from Mr. H. Washington by Howard Saffold.

The Du Sable Museum of African American History hereby accepts the property under the conditions specified above.

Dated this __10th__ day of __NOVEMBER__, 19__92__

DU SABLE MUSEUM OF AFRICAN AMERICAN HISTORY

By _____

Please sign both copies of the Deed of Gift form and return them to the Du Sable Museum of African

Earlier I said I appreciate being remembered for the work that I do. The certificate below is one example.

CHAPTER 13

POSITIVE ANTI-CRIME THRUST

There is nothing more important for the African American community today than to take the initiative in addressing the problem of incarceration and physical and mental debilitation of that population.

Retirement for me does not mean "sitting down." Instead, it means standing up for causes and exerting energy to make the way for coming generations. In order to relate to young people, I must remember that I too was young. Looking back on those early days of my life enables me to communicate with adolescents in a meaningful way.

After 25 years of service with the Chicago Police Department and being Chief of Executive Security for two Mayors of the City of Chicago, I am eager to use the skills that I have acquired over the years in the most meaningful way. To sum up my experiences, I have served as a Beat Officer, School Officer, and Gang Crime Investigator. I have also worked in Mass Transit, Public Housing, Neighborhood Relations, Special Operations, and Dignitary Protection.

My work gave me familiarity with all areas of the City of Chicago. I have also worked in national programs, and I have performed my duties in international settings.

I have dedicated my time to the organization that we founded in 1979, The Positive Anti-Crime Thrust. Inc. (PACT). I serve as President and CEO. PACT is the programmatic arm of the Afro-American Patrolman's League, focused on activism and implementation of programs that target community control of police. As our experience has grown, so too has our mission. Recognizing the interdependencies of Police, Courts and Corrections, their influence and impact on the African-American community, and further, the lack of a cohesive community approach to addressing concerns and issues within these institutions, PACT has developed a holistic strategy of redress. One thermometer that measures the success of the organization is the feedback that we get from others.

We as a society have witnessed and allowed the police by way of the justice system to become overseers of the Black family relative to our basic human rights which, if left uncorrected, can destroy the future of our children. When we as Black police officers began to raise these contradictions in the 1960's, we had not counted on being isolated, resisted and attacked by entities such as police unions. We stood on the police department's own code of ethics and the United States Constitution.

The majority of white people including white police officers see and have been seeing the same inconsistencies that we have. The silence from the majority community on this issue has had a devastating reverse impact on America's economy in particular. Therefore, collaborating to rescue Black youth from the vicious cycle of the juvenile and adult justice system would be a righteous thing to do.

Finally, on the subject of Police Accountability…who other than the decent police officers themselves are expected to blow that whistle? Do we honestly expect community residents are more courageous than the police are about telling the truth when dangerous people are involved? A few honest officers of all ranks and races, speaking out against evil practices could be a great encouragement to their peers as well as so many intimidated families that include the future leaders of this country.

Most police officers, if they would dare admit to the truth, are aware of who amongst them are in need of special training or have psychological or substance abuse problems. They know these individuals are more prone to commit cowardly acts, acts of hatefulness toward certain groups because of their race, gender, ethnicity or sexual orientation. They know who commit thefts and other more serious types of crime. We learn about them as early as the training academy or by observing them on the streets over a short period of time. We usually know the repeat offenders and which individuals are administratively or politically connected.

So many decent officers are forced or compromised into underserved loyalty just by accepting fruits of the crime, (it only takes one time), being allowed to congregate with the so-called shot callers, many being crooked politicians, union reps, and immediate superiors. The majority of decent men and women in this honorable profession have suffered in silence for so long it is probably causing some to retire as early as possible or change careers out of frustration. It is too bad that public confidence and safety has to be sacrificed because the big group of good people allows a little group of unscrupulous people to run it.

In order to change the paradigm, we must take action to break barricades to progress. I therefore speak out on issues that impede justice and equality. A recent *Chicago Defender* article revealed findings from an examination of the (FOP) Fraternal Order of Police. FOP is the official collective bargaining agent for Chicago police officers. The examination of the FOP contract contains a "Bill of Rights" of which the highly controversial articles 6.1-6.12 and 8.1-8.8 govern the discipline of police officers.

The Chicago *Defender* article further charges that the inaction by the City of Chicago to prosecute police officers who have committed crimes against citizens is in part due to the inadequate clauses in the contract. The City Council has had opportunities to review the contract but has not done so. In some instances, aldermen have complained about the FOP contract that they approved themselves (Hare, 2016, Jan 7).

I supplied a commentary to the article in the following words:

"The Positive Anti-Crime Thrust applauds this very significant article. It points all interested and affected parties to the root of a recurring systemic problem in Chicago. Please know if you do not act on this notice, please shut up, hold your peace and bleed peacefully. The Positive Anti-Crime Thrust does not have that luxury. We are committed to help any organized self-help effort for long term change". Howard Saffold (Saffold, 2016, Jan.8).

Another issue on which I had earlier expressed my views was the Jon Burge case. My comments were recorded in a WBEZ (91.5 blog) posted July 1, 2010:

"My first reaction to the verdict was that it was a slow justice, but a justice nonetheless in a case that was so egregious it had put the whole justice system on trial. The jury is still out on whether or not the justice system will ever be viewed without skepticism from the public's perspective because of the time lag from the initial complaint [of torture] until the final adjudication." As noted in the blog, I went on to commend the federal government for mounting a perjury and obstruction of justice prosecution when all avenues of indictment for the torture itself were precluded by the statute of limitations. By contrast, the Cook County State's Attorney's Office had been convicted along with Burge. It various leaders, particularly Richard Daley and Ricardo Devine, knew, or should have known, the injustice being inflicted by Burge and his colleagues. PACT takes action to inform and reform. To inform we publicize this warning:

CERN

CORRUPTION
EXCESSIVE FORCE
RACIAL DISCRIMINATION
NEPOTISM

Youth, especially Black males, are targeted by police as a new economic commodity to promote the criminal and juvenile justice system. Police are serving as the new slave catchers. The Court is the Auction Center (Few trials, mostly plea bargains) lots of bonds, fines and forfeitures.

The Jails & Prisons (facilitate the adaptation to being told by overseers when and how to come and go).

The economic outcomes produced by this system are how you as a commodity are valued or devalued.

The art of unfair politics often decides at what level of the game your elected or self-appointed representatives are allowed to play. You pay dearly when you fail to protect your own interest. People must be held accountable when the table stakes include your resources, especially your freedom.

To reform, PACT is further advocating the following:

STEM (Science, Technology, Engineering and Math)

- Quality education for youth to interrupt the constant flow from the schoolhouse to incarceration.
- Inner city youth involvement in quality STEM training is one of PACT's major components for the next few years. Engaging inner city youth and their families in technology training will prepare them for jobs and allow them to join Chicago's STEM workforce that is growing in leaps and bounds annually.
- CPS is in process of establishing digital literacy standards for CPS students to meet before graduation. STEM training is necessary or the graduation rates will get lower than they already are.

EMPLOYMENT

- A second major PACT focus is employment for challenged youth and their families. PACT has drafted an entrepreneurship/small business model that needs refinement and resources.
- Where are the jobs in Chicago: private sector, government?

How PACT will contribute to the "stop the violence" in Chicago and beyond.

- Investing in education will lead to economic advancement that will lead to public safety that will impact positively the violence in the city.
- Sangamon County has developed a comprehensive public safety model that connects legislation, education, entrepreneurship, and other common-good areas of life. With proper resources, PACT can develop this kind of model tailored to meet the needs of Cook and larger counties in the state and beyond. This type of model is necessary because Cook County has more incarcerated citizens than all of the other counties in the state; one of the highest in the nation!
  - Social media will be a major component in implementing this model.
  - Funding will also be needed.

FUTURE STEPS

1. Stakeholders from all four levels of government will be involved—actively participating in addressing this long time crises—youth violence in Chicago.
2. Downsizing the jails with integrity and insight into what is needed to support this process to advance all involved.

3. Greater understanding of TIF monies in order to direct resources to proper channels.
4. Collaborations among Illinois counties.
5. Creation of apps for teaching STEM concepts to primary grade students.

It is shameful that we don't have very much core leadership to take up the gauntlet of Harold Washington and Martin Luther King, but that is not a reason to despair. I am encouraged by the recent enthusiasm of young people in protesting the police killings around the nation and particularly here in Chicago. I am pleased to be an elder who has been summoned to the table to share information with young enthusiasts. I am happy to pass on the truths that we discovered in Discrimination Law Suit where we won a victory over the City of Chicago. I know the formula that Harold Washington used to be successful and can offer some points on politics. In my retirement years, I gain energy when I see kids avoiding the pitfalls and becoming successful adults. I am reinvigorated when our message is received by those who are incarcerated and to follow the progress of ones who are released and do not return to a criminal lifestyle. I am still committed to the civil rights struggle and have high hopes for the future generations.

HOWARD SAFFOLD

Historical Highlights

1979 1983 1990 1996 1997 1998 2001 2002 2003 2007 2009

1979

The Positive Anti-Crime Thrust, Inc. is founded as the programmatic component of the Afro-American Patrolman's League with the goal of working to reduce the incarceration and recidivism rates exploding in the African-American urban centers.

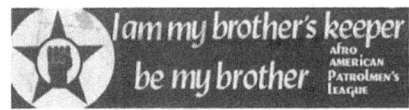

1983

Prison Reform Advocacy Yardstick is formed (PRAY). This group, composed of many faith based institutions, was developed as an advocacy consortium focused on prison related issues.

1990

Ako-Ben Nyame Nwu Na Mawu Society formed as a counterpoint to gang culture. This was one of PACT's initial efforts at developing a program that informed young men of their broader African culture and encouraged them to be protectors of their communites rather than a souce of confusion and even danger. The symbols of PACT's logo include the symbols represented by the name of the society:

Akoben is the symbol of vigilance and wariness. Akoben is a horn used to sound a battle cry.

Nyame Nwu Na Mawu is the symbol of God's omnipresence and the perpetual existence of man's spirit This signifies the immortality of man's soul, believed to be a part of God. Because the soul rests with God after death, it cannot die.

Return to Top

1996

Operation Safe Bet started in 1996 in one Chicago area high school, soon expanding to three and eventually eight. Its focus was the retention, retrieval and academic engagement of at-risk teens through a combination of activities geared toward lifestyle and life approach modification.

While a template was used for each school program, uniqueness of the specific school was taken into consideration in the design and implementation methodology. After program design and administration sign off, the Security Specialist team implemented the program, engaging the client population. Students were referred to the "Safe Bet Officer" based on several criteria:

- Retrieval of students dropped from the official school rolesAbsenteeism
- Gang Intervention
- Behavior/Discipline
- Academic Performance Issues
- Personal / Other (i.e. lack of motivation, family issues, incarceration, etc.)

The Safe Bet Officers were unanimous in the positive view of the programs and a key success metric was a 70% retrieval/retained rate for this at-risk population (clearly a positive considering that from the total incoming African American male freshmen in 1994, 67% failed to graduate within five years).

Sidebar:

Home
News and Events
Programs
Prison Ministry
Research Links
Our Partners

Police
Courts
Corrections

P.A.C.T. Presents Video Webzine

P.A.C.T. NEWS UPDATE:
Positive Anti-Crime Thrust, Inc. develops three new web tools to assist in delivering relevant community safety and criminal justice community. Vimeo for video, and a new blog and Facebook presence for topical content.

POLICE, PRISONS, POLITICS, & POWER I

1997

Project DETours at-risk-youth and prisoner interaction launches. DETours took Chicago youth on tours inside jails and prisons where they interacted with prisoners in planned activities that provide realistic insights into the negative lifestyles and conditions within the penal system. Originally focused on delivering service to youth living in Chicago Housing Authority developments, by 2004 the program was focused on targeting youth provided through a variety of private and government agencies in greater Chicago.

Return to Top

1998

Youth Enhancement Strategy (Y.E.S.) program developed. The youth enhancement strategy incorporates several programs that are focused on reducing the involvement and engagement of inner-city youth with the criminal justice system. While each program has been implemented at various times over the years, and each carries its own success history, they are all incorporated in one strategy and targeted to run concurrently as on-going tactics to reduce youth incarceration and those behaviors that lead to it. Y.E.S. Program goals:

- Through direct program development decrease the drop-out rate in the Chicago metro area
- Improve safety/security and thus the learning environment in public schools
- Reduce youth incarceration and negative interaction with the criminal justice system

2001

Recognizing the devastating impact the criminal justice system has on individuals, families and communities, and the limited understanding and resources available to address issues and propose/implement practical solutions, the Prison Ministry Network (PMN) was formed.

Comprised of many veteran prison volunteers, key church prison ministry volunteers, community activists and legal/law enforcement professionals, this "consortium" of organizations and individuals has three key goals:

- Develop the potential within churches and their prison ministries to deliver meaningful and practical services to at risk youth, incarcerated adults/youth and the newly released, as well as their families/support structures.
- Research and Understand the issues within the prison system and the effects on our community.
- Advocate both directly and in association with like-minded churches, other faith based institutions and organizations, for changes that we deem necessary.

Return to Top

2002

Community-Police Relations Information Center project kicks off. This pilot program was an online system for documenting official misconduct complaints. The primary purpose of the database was to provide the community with accurate information on various aspects of misconduct in their neighborhoods, and use that information in their efforts at community policing. A second use was planned for independent research by criminal justice educational facilities throughout the country.

Return to Top

2003

"Train the Trainer" curriculum development for IDOC inmates initiated with Chicago City Colleges and Roosevelt University.

2007

PACT initializes Leadership Development project, Community Organizing 101. Partnering with Safer Foundation and Kennedy-King College (A City College of Chicago) the course focused on the twin objectives of decreasing receitvism among a targeted group of newly released individuals, and developing the capacity of those individuals to participate as trainers.

Return to Top

2009

In order to facilitated the development of entrepreneurial skills in the ex-offender population, especially the graduates of PACT's Community Organizing 101 program, PACT starts a for profit company, Self-Help Inspired People, LLC (SHIP). Initially SHIP will facilitate the development of a fresh produce distribution capacity and a consultancy focused on the customization and implementation of programs for troubled youth.

With a long history of successful program development and implementation, our current focus is on three major areas:

- **Community/Police Relations** As strong believers in community justice, we are committed to the development and implementations of programs that enhance community control of their public safety.
- **Equal Justice Under Law** We work to enhance the fair disbursement of justice and advocate positions on laws that adversely and/or positively affect our community. Further, as information driven organization, we educate the community to enhance their understanding of the law and their rights.
- **Prisons and "Corrections"** There must be a "corrections" or rehabilitation component to our prison system. A major strategy thrust for PACT is to reduce recidivism, and its dramatic impact on community safety, by partnering with like- minded organizations and institutions on a holistic approach to education and self-development within the prison population. (PACT,2012)

The recent report from Loyola University and Hull house and it observation that while the vast majority of drug users are white, the vast majority of those imprisoned for drug crimes are

Black, only serves as the most recent evidence that "something is wrong."

While we may not have all the answers, two things we are sure of; there is no quick fix and there is no fix at all if we do not do it ourselves. At PACT, we believe the most valuable thing we can do is serve as an information resource, both to serve the community with factual information they can use to address existing bureaucratic institutions and to educate our political leaders. We also strongly believe that we must hold our leaders accountable for what they do (or don't do) to address practices within the criminal justice system that impacts on our very survival.

An excerpt from a *Chicago Defender* article explained the focus of our organization:

> "Saffold says that education is key in curbing crime in the inner city. Education, like a pendulum, he believes, swings both ways." He states, 'Our focus is to empower the community through education and referral services. We must educate people in the community concerning their rights as citizens and as voters. We must educate and train officers on cultural differences, how to engage members in the community in a positive way through partnership and respect.' In addition to working with experts in law enforcement, education, mental health and spiritual counselors, Saffold's organization works to bring law enforcement and community residents together in workshops, meetings and discussions during times of relative peace" (Chicago Defender article, 2003, Nov. 15).

REFERENCES

Abc7Chicago. (2008, Jan. 26). Former Mayor Eugene Sawyer remembered. Retrieved on http://abc7chicago.com/arhive/5916709/.

Alkalimat, A. & Gills, D. (1989). *Harold Washington and the Crisis of Black Power in Chicago: Mass Protest.* Twenty-First Century Books and Publications. Chicago, IL.

An, S. (2015, Dec. 10) Former interim mayor talks about the politics behind the succession process at city hall. *WBEZ91.5 Chicago.* Retrieved on http://www.wbez.org/news/former-interim-mayor-talks-about-politics-behind-succession-process-city-hall-114133

Black, T. (2003). *Bridges of Memory.* "Interview with Leroy Martin" Evanston: University Press.

Brian. Interview with Howard Saffold (1997, Feb. 17). Video by Shaka. Chicago, IL.

Cheryl Means, et al. vs. City of Chicago. No. 81 C 2988. Saffold, H. Deposition. (1983, Nov. 11).

Chicago History Makers Oral Interview with Howard Saffold (2002, June 5) Larry Crowe, interviewer. Chicago, Illinois.

Chicago History Makers Oral Interview with Howard Saffold (2004, Dec. 20) Gloria Swanson, interviewer. Chicago, Illinois.

Chicago Police Department Summary Investigation Report of C.R. # 59321. Accused: Bigby& Saffold. (1972, April 26).

Chicago Police Department Complaint Review Panel Hearing of CR 599321, (1972, Oct. 2). Accused: Bigby& Saffold. Star: 11920 & 11881. Unit: Cabrini Green 091.

Cruz vs. Bilandic et al. Deposition of Howard Saffold. No. 77 C 217980. (1980, Dec. 22).

Davis, R. (1989) The Death of Mayor Harold Washington. *Chicago Tribune*. Retrieved from http://www.chicagotribune.com/news/nationworld/politics/chicagodays-haroldwashingtondeath-story-story.html.

Dodd, B. R. (1988, Dec. 25). Sawyer puts hopes in hands of a gambler. *Chicago Tribune*. News. Retrieved from http://articles.chicagotribune.com/1988-12-25/news/8802270133_1_first-black-mayor-political-consultant-New-Orleans.

Dulaney. Interview with Howard Saffold (2009, July 27). Chicago, IL.

Fitzsimmons, E. (2998, January 27). Former mayor Eugene Sawyer paved road back to civility, mourners recall. *Chicago Tribune*. Retrieved from http://articles.Chicagotribune.com/2008-01-27/news/0801260385.

Gibson, E. (1988) "Where Do We Go from Here/ Harold Washington and the Future." In H. J. Young, Ed. *The Black Church and the Harold Washington Story*. Chicago: Wyndham Press.

Hare, K. (2016, Jan. 7) Fraternal Order of Police-Is the tail wagging the dog? *Chicago Defender*. Retrieved from http://chicagodefender.com/2016/01/07/fraternal-order-of-police/

Johnson, D. (1987, Nov. 26) Chicago's Mayor Harold Washington Dies after a Heart Attack in His Office. *New York Times*. Retrieved from http://www.nytimes.com/1987 obituaries/

Martin, H. (1988). "Eulogy of Mayor Harold Washington." In H. J. Young, Ed. *The Black Church and the Harold Washington Story*. Chicago: Wyndham Press.

Miller, A. (1989). Harold Washington the mayor, the man. Chicago: Bonus Books.

Miller, A. (1989). "The Final Day." *Chicago Tribune* Final Edition, Section: Sunday Magazine.

McClory, R. (1970). *The Man Who Beat Clout City.* Chicago: The Swallow Press Inc. National Association of Human Rights. (1980). Interview with Howard Saffold.

McClory, R. (1996, Apr. 18). Freedom fighter. *Chicago Reader.* News and Politics Feature.
   Retrieved from http://chicagodefender.com/2016/01/07/fraternal-order-of-police/

Nolan, P. (2011). *Campaign/The 1983 Election That Rocked Chicago.* Northfield, IL: Amika Press.

PACT Positive Anti-Crime Thrust). (2012) Retrieved from http://communitysafety.org/.

Pat, L. (2003, Nov. 15). Nonprofit unifies cops, community. *Chicago Defender.* Retrieved from http://www.highbeam.com.

Reddick, G. (1988). "Harold Washington/ A Call to Economic Development." In H. J. Young, Ed. *The Black Church and the Harold Washington Story.* Chicago: Wyndham Press.

Saffold, H. (2016, Jan. 8) Commentary on article: Fraternal Order of Police-Is the tail wagging the dog? Chicago Defender. Retrieved from http://chicagodefender.com/2016/01/07/fraternal-order-of-police/

Saffold, H. (1985). "Final Project" University Without Walls Program, Chicago, IL.

Saffold vs City of Chicago. (1991, Aug. 26). 775 F. Supp. 1126 (N.D. 111. 1991) U.S. District Court for the Northern District of Illinois.

Sneed, M. & O'Malley, K. (1985, Oct. 11). Chicago Tribune News.

Sneed, M. & O'Malley, K. (1986, Sept. 8). Chicago Tribune News.

The Chicago Metropolitan Agency for Planning, 2007). City of Chicago Affirmative Action Plan. Retrieved from http://www.cmap.illinois.gov/

The People of the State of Illinois vs. Howard Saffold. E 985647 E985648 Branch 5. (April 29, 1976).

Wright, J. (1988). "Church Growth and Political Empowerment/ The Significance of Harold Washington." In H. J. Young, Ed. The Black Church and the Harold Washington Story. Chicago: Wyndham Hall Press.

Listing of Payroll Deductions for Afro-American League- pay period 3/15/80.

This Roster is a copy of the actual list of our members who were signed up to pay dues every 1st and 15th of each month. The Gross amount from each member three (3) dollars per payday. That was a total of over (25) twenty-five hundred dollars every two weeks. That money paid our monthly rent, utility bills and a portion of other expenses required for our non-profit organization. The ranks of the members ranged from patrol officers to detective or youth officer up to and including sergeants of police.

The names on this historical list are the men and women who were brave enough to withstand the opposition from within the department by openly declaring to identify themselves and commit their financial support an organization that spoke out against police misconduct, racial and sexual discrimination in hiring practices. They were advocates for police accountability during a time in Chicago's history, that being on this list could adversely affect your upward mobility as well as your entire career on the Chicago Police Department. Nothing we ever accomplished would have been possible without the involvement of these brave souls. Our collective thanks and prayers go out to friends and families of them all.

Author's personal note: I know that many have made their transition at the time publication. I offer my deepest condolences, to each and every one, as appropriate.

AFRO-AMERICAN PATROLMAN'S LEAGUE ROSTER

Abbey, Mitchell J.
Abington, Eugene
Abram, Paul W.
Adams, Lloyd J.
Adams, Stanley
Adkins, Lemonie
Akins, Robert Jr.
Albert, Joseph W.
A.Bailey, Ronald
Alfred, Glenn E.

Allen, Calvin E.
Alston, Emmitt A.
Alston, Lonnie
Alston, William D.
Alston, Ronald
Amos, Alvin
Anderson, Alan P.
Anderson, B.
Anderson, E. B.
Anderson, Gene A.
Anderson, J.

Archibald, Abe
Armstead, Earl
Armstrong, R. J.
Arnold, L. D.
Atwood, Fletcher
Avant, Bernard
Averyhart, W. E.
Alexander, J.
Alford, James E.
Baker, Curtis R.
Baker, Clinton R.
Banks, Leon
Barksdale, David
Barksdale, Jiles
Barksdale, R. L.
Barlow, Ladys L.
Barnes, Frank R.
Barnett, C.
Barron, John D.
Batom, Patricia A.
Battle, Milton
Batts, William Jr.

Anderson, John E.
Anderson, R. G.
Anderson, T. A. Jr.
Anderson, T. Jr.
Andrews, M. C.
Anguiano, Lillian
Anthony, Michael
Archer, W. A. Jr.
Benton, Major Jr.
Berry, Warren E.
Bigby, W. C. Jr.
Bitoy, Lucio M. Jr.
Black, Quentin C.
Blackman, John E.
Blair, Leon C.
Blaye, Joseph G.
Blount, Lamar
Bolling, Thomas W.
Bonds, C. B. Jr.
Bone, Edward M.
Bonner, Robert
Borders, Everett
Boston, Lamonte J.
Bottom, Donald
Bowman, R. M.
Boyd, Diane
Boyd, Eddie L.
Boyd, Lebert L.
Boynes, Mechell D.
Bradley, Bruce V.
Bradshaw, L. W. Jr.
Brady, Fred Jr.

Beach, Agene
Beal, Michael D.
Bechom, Jessie Jr.
Bell, Barbara A.
Bell, Ernest L.
Bell, Kenneth
Benford, Horace G.
Bennett, Doretha
Brooks, Charles L.
Brooks, Cornell
Brooks, E.
Broughton, B.
Browder, Arthur D.
Brown, Anthony N.
Brown, Andrew Jr.
Brown, David
Brown, Deborah E.
Brown, Frank A. Jr.
Brown, Henry Jr.
Brown, Henry C.
Brown, Kenneth
Brown, Lorna M.
Brown, Maurice E.
Brown, Merle E.
Brown, Norbert A.
Brown, Vernon A.
Bryant, Phillip R.
Buckles, Leslie
Buckley, Pamela J.
Buckner, William H.
Buick, Brenda
Buick, W. E. Jr.

Branch, Fredrick
Brandon, Matthew
Bratton, L. L.
Bridges, David
Britt, Lawrence
Britton, Lawler

Cage, Frank C. Jr.
Calhoun, Donnell
Campbell, John
Campbell, Samuel
Campbell, William
Caridine, Eddie
Carpenter, John A.
Carter, Charles E.
Carter, Colbert L.
Carter, Freddie
Cartwright, A. E.
Cartwright, George R.
Cates, Jennie E.
Chaffee, Eugene
Chambliss, Charles
Chapman, Jerome
Cheatham, L. B.
Chisen, James L.
Chisholm, R. H.
Chrismon, Morris
Clark, Lawrence
Clay, Carol A.
Clay, Edgar
Clay, Lemuel
Clay, Willie L.

Burdette, Ronald
Burdine, Dorice
Burke, M. J.
Burton, Henry P.
Butler, D. J.
Butler, James H.
Butts, Leon D.
Cobb, W.C. Jr.
Cochran, Willie B.
Cole, Louis C.
Collier, James
Collins, A. L.
Collins, Brenda
Collins, D. D.
Compton, Arthur C.
Conley, Charles G.
Conner, Stephen
Cook, Larry
Cook, Robert H. Jr.
Copeland, Andre L.
Cotton, Charles E.
Cotton, James E.
Coulter, Isaac Jr.
Cox, Albert Jr.
Cox, Kenneth O.
Cox, Velma
Craig, James W.
Craig, Law B. Jr
Crawford, Ronald
Crawford, S. J.
Crawley, J. L. Jr.
Crayton, Herman J.

Cleaton, Darryl
Clemons, Hosie L
Coates, Freeman J.
Coats, Charles
Cobb, Gilbert J.
Cobb, W. H. Jr.

Crossley, Hosea H.
Croswell, J. A.
Crowley, Henry L.
Crump, Henry E.
Crutch, Robert L.
Cunningham, F. Jr.

Daniels, T. D.
Davenport, J.
David, Carey H.
Davis, Allan
Davis, Arthur L.
Davis, Elias
Davis, George D.
Davis, Mark A.
Davis, Robert L.
Davis, Ronald E.
Davis, Ronald S.
Davis, Stephen L.
Davis, Theo E. Jr.
Davis, Theodore R.
Davis, W. H. Jr.
Dawson, Charles E.
De White, N. W.
Dewitt, Ralph E.

Crenshaw, J. C.
Crisler, Curtis
Crooks, James R.
Crosby, I. E. Jr.
Cross, Herman Jr.
Crossley, H. H. Jr.

Dotson, Jerry A.
Doty, Robert H.
Downing, Anthony
Doyle, Clifford

Eaglin, P. R.
Echols, Julius P
Eckles, Fred Jr.
Edmond, Herman
Edmondsen, C. E.
Edwards, C. N.
Edwards, Robert L.
Elliott, M. A.
Elliott, Valerie
Ellis, Douglas Jr.
Ellison, Jethell
Ely, Roosevelt
Elzy, Louis C. Jr.
Embry, William A.
Ervin, John C. Jr.
Evans, Nelson E.
Ezell, Artis

Fairmon, Rosetta
Fason, John W.

Deal, James D.
Dease, Joe
Dickerson, E. L.
Digby, Robert L.
Dishman, T.
Dix, Lawrence III
Dones, Wilman
Frazier, Jesse
Freeman, Henry C.
Fuqua, Donald S.

Gadberry, Oliver
Gaines, Ronald
Gaiter, Booker T.
Galimore, Louis
Garland, Quenton
Garmon, Jerry
Garner, Michael
Garrison, Jerome
Gary, Charles
German, Earl D.
Gholar, John H.
Gibson, Daniel A.
Giles, Beverly A.
Giles, C. D. Jr.
Gilmore, C. A.
Gilmore, C. C. Jr.
Glees, Henry
Godbold, Glen
Goode, Samuel
Goosby, F. G.
Gordon, Joyce P.

Felix, Kenneth
Ferguson, C. D.
Fitzpatrick, C. W.
Flanagan, Norman
Flanagan, T.
Foster, Darnell
Frazier, Gregory
Greene, Jesse L.
Greenlee, George
Greenlee, K.
Greenwood, E. G.
Gregory, D. Jr.
Gregory, John
Griffin, Clifford
Griffin, Cleo Jr.
Griffin, E. T.
Griffin, James L.
Grissett, James K.
Grizzard, Kenneth
Grymes, M. U.
Guess, Wendell J.
Gwin, Richard S.

Haire, Alfred C.
Hale, Robert S.
Haley, Bill
Hall, Fred
Ham, Phyllis A.
Hamilton, Charles E.
Hamilton, Noreen
Hansberry, Edward L.
Hardy, Judge F.

Gordon, Ronald J.
Gordon, William A.
Gosa, Edgar L.
Grant, Gregory S.
Grant, Henry Jr.
Grant, Leroy O.
Green, Levern
Greene, D. T.
Harris, William E.
Harrold, Arthur E.
Hart, Aaron A.
Hart, John J.
Hartfield, Noel C.
Hartford, Uless B.
Hawkins, Charles A.
Hawkins, G. L.
Hawthorne, A.
Hayes, Alonzo L.
Hayes, C. W. Jr.
Hayes, Raymond L.
Hayes, Rodney
Haynes, E. D.
Haynes, James E.
Haywood, Artis
Heard, Albert
Height, Ida M.
Henderson, A. H.
Henderson, F. A. Jr.
Henderson, M. L.
Henley, John E.
Herron, Samuel
High, Ocie R.

Harper, James R.
Harper, Willie W.
Harris, Arthur E.
Harris, Carl M.
Harris, Charles
Harris, Elijah
Harris, G. S.
Harris, Otis B.
Hinkson, Dennis D.
Hite, Abraham Jr.
Hobbs, E. J.
Hockett, Cecil M.
Hodges, Eddie L.
Hodrick, Joyce
Hogan, Johnny
Hollins, Percy
Holmes, Arthur
Holmes, Calvin
Holton, Hubert
Horton, Frank M.
Houser, Alan
Howard, Alaus L.
Howard, P. D.
Howell, Alton P.
Huff, Roger W.
Hunt, Edward
Hunt, Joann
Hunter, Roland
Hunter, S. Jr.

Irwin, Frank Jr.

Hightower, W. J.
Hill, Lawrence
Hill, Reginald
Hines, Jack P.
Hines, Paula C.
Jackson, Henry W.
Jackson, Isaac
Jackson, Laurence
Jackson, Renard
James, William M.
Jamison, Ernest
Jamison, Wilbur
Jemerson, Willie
Jenkins, A. L. Jr.
Jenkins, Joseph S.
Johns, Frank H.
Johnson, David M.
Johnson, Earl L.
Johnson, Eugene
Johnson, Everett
Johnson, Forest
Johnson, James
Johnson, Jerry
Johnson, Joanna
Johnson, Joellyn
Johnson, Johnny
Johnson, Joseph J.
Johnson, Leroy Jr.
Johnson, McHenry
Johnson, M. L.
Johnson, Michael
Johnson, Ray W.

Jackson, A. J. Sr.
Jackson, Curtis H.
Jackson, David
Jackson, G. W. S.
Jackson, Gregory
Jones, Benjamin
Jones, Curtis
Jones, Eddie
Jones, Godfrey E.
Jones, James W.
Jones, Jennifer
Jones, Johnny
Jones, Samuel
Jones, William H.
Joseph, P. E.
Joyner, Ruth M

Keith, Clarence E.
Kelley, Anthony H.
Kelley, Charles D.
Kiley, Barbara
Kimber, Arthur
King, Eddie Jr.
King, Sylvester A.
King, Tommie E.
Kirk, Alfred Jr.

Lacey, Sammy Jr.
Landrum, Elves
Langston, R. L.
Layne, Frederick
Lee, Donald A.

Johnson, Robert E.
Johnson, R.
Johnson, Rollins
Jones, Arties

Leftridge, P. G.
Lemon, Robert A.
Leonard, Thomas J.
Lewis, Charles S.
Lewis, C.
Lewis, Clarence
Lewis, Elmer
Lightfoot, William G.
Lilly, James R.
Lindsay, G. A.
Linzy, James A.
Lipsey, Henry Jr.
Littleton, John
Locke, Billy G.
Lockett, S. E. III
Longley, Clarence
Longstreet, E. W.
Lyles, George E.
Lyles, Phillip O.
McClinton, D.
Mack, William R.
Mackey, Horace Jr.
Madison, C. J.
Madkin, Esquel
Mangrum, Earl R.
Mann, Kenneth E.
Mann, Marie D.

Lee, Frank K.
Lee, James S.
Lee, Lamar S.
Lee, Mary E.

Marshall, T.
Martin, Donald E.
Martin, Doris I.
Martin, Harley
Martin, Leroy
Mason, Henry Jr.
Massey, Marshall
Mastin, Barry
Matthews, Elliot A.
Matthews, H. C.
Matthews, John C.
Maury, Marvin A.
Mays, Harry M.
McCadd, Frederick
McCaster, M. L.
McClain, John T.
McClellan, R. A.
McClendon, Franci
McClendon, Elton

McCloud, James Jr.
McCoy, Donald R.
McCray, James
McCully, Walter J.
McDowell, R. B.
McDowell, R Jr.
McEwen, E. R. Jr.

Mann, Thomas J.
Marbury, J. O. Jr.
Markham, W. T.
Marshall, Kevin K.

McGowan, Norman, E.
McGruder, John Jr.
McKay, Ralph
McKeever, Robert
McKelphin, Cleve
McKnight, John R.
McLaurin, W. A.
McLendon, J. B.
McLin, Robert N.
McMikel, H. T. Jr.
McNair, Maceo M.
McNeil, Kenneth
Meadows, G. E.
Meredith, James A.
Merriwether, J. R.
Meyers, Ronald W.
Mial, Paul D.
Miller, Aundre L.
Miller, Glenn E.
Miller, Robert E. Jr.
Miller, Russell O.
Mills, Raymond S.
Mills, W. B. Jr.
Minniefield, B.
Mitchell, J. H.
Mitchell, R. J. Jr.

McGaha, R.
McGavock, Garvis
McGinnis, Jerome
McGowan, Bennett

Montrel, Delores
Moore, Booker
Moore, C.
Moore, Curtis
Moore, Donald A.
Moore, Richard M.
Moore, Theopsy
Morgan, B. A. Jr.
Morgan, Cherif A.
Morgan, Lorenzo
Morgan, Michael E.
Morris, William G.
Morrissette, G.
Morton, Arthur
Morton, James A.
Morton, Phyliss J
Moses, Edward Jr.
Muse, Alfred L.
Myers, Beverly V.

Neal, Willie James
Nelson, Derrick
Nelson, Lewis
Nowlin, James R.

O'Shield, Leroy
Ogletree, W. Jr.

Mitchell, Thomas
Modeste, Gregory
Monegain, L. L.
Montgomery, P.
Montgomery, R.
Palmer, Otto W.
Parker, William A.
Parker, W. L.
Parks, Earl J.
Parks, Robert J.
Parram, Ronald L.
Parrott, Frank L.
Pates, Henry M.
Patterson, Johnny
Patterson, W. L.
Patton, John W.
Payne, Kenneth
Payne, Vernon L.
Penn, Willie L.
Peoples, John
Pepper, Phillip E.
Perisee, Virgil S.
Perkins, Gregory
Perkins, Walter I.
Peters, Frankie A.
Peyton, Ralph J.
Phillips, Nathan
Pickens, Tyrone L.
Pickett, James Jr.
Pierce, Carol L.
Pierce, Kenneth R.
Pierce, Wilbur Jr.

Ogletree, W. F. Jr.
Orr, Charles
Overstreet, M. E.
Owens, George A.
Owens, M. O. Jr.
Porter, Richard
Portis, Camelia A
Portlock, L. M.
Powell, Melvin
President, Obia H.
Price, Paul E.
Price, Richard A.
Primous, Albert D.
Primous, William W.
Proctor, William
Pruitt, L. Z.
Pulliam, Edward L

Rachal, Frank A.
Radney, H. L.
Ramsey, A. Jr.
Ramsey, Charles H.
Ray, Clausell
Raymond, Clyde W.
Redding, Charles
Redmond, Will
Redwell, E.
Reese, Thomas J.
Reynolds, Edward Jr.
Rhue, Stephen C.
Richardson, C.
Richardson, D. E.

Pittman, Dexter E.
Pointer, Howard
Porter, Bernard
Porter, Thomas H.
Ricks, Frank Jr.
Ricks, R. J. Jr.
Ridley, Horace E.
Rivers, James E.
Roberts, Jean A.
Robinson, A. Jr.
Robertson, F. L.
Robinson, Herman
Robinson, Joel L.
Roby, George C.
Rochon, A. C.
Rockymore, Lionel
Roebuck, L. R.
Rogers, L. D.
Rogers, Lloyd W.
Rogers, William A.
Roseman, Danny
Ross, Lorrell G.
Ross, William B.
Rowe, Albert J.
Rowland, Cisco D.
Rudd, Ronald
Rutherford, C, N.

Sanders, Joseph M.
Sanders, Stanley
Sandifer, John C.
Sanlin, Robert Jr.

JesseRichardson, L.
Richardson, M.
Richardson, P. O.
Richardson, W.
Seals, Leonard W.
Sebastian, S.
Senior, Curtis
Shackelford, M. E.
Sharp, Tyrone
Shavers, Conrad
Shaw, Mose D.
Shaw, William Jr.
Shead, Brenda J.
Shepard, Don E.
Sheperd, E. N.
Sherley, Ulas
Sherman, Mari F.
Shields, J. R.
Shields, John H.
Shotwell, R.
Shumpert, Everett
Sias, Charles L.
Sias, Harry L.
Silas, Nathan E.
Simmons, Roscoe C.
Sims, Austin L.
Skyles, Patricia
Slappey, Barry
Slaughter, Ronald
Sledd, Yvonne
Sledge, A. Jr.
Smiley, Richard L.

Saunders, Willie
Savage, Carl D. Jr.
Scott, William
Smith, Elliott H.
Smith, F. D.
Smith, Garnell
Smith, J. O.
Smith, James
Smith, Jimmie
Smith, John L.
Smith, John L.
Smith, Kenneth G.
Smith, Lawrence H.
Smith, Lillard L.
Smith, Marva D.
Smith, Milton H.
Smith, Norman E.
Smith, Phillip
Smith, Robert B.
Smith, Robert F.
Smith, Ronald C.
Smith, Roy Van
Smith, Steve R.
Smith, Willie B.
Smith, Willie J.
Smith, Willie J.
Snowden, R. A. Jr.
Soil, Van T.
Sostand, Clavon
Southerland, T. B.
Spaulding, M. C.
Spencer, Barbara

Smith, Allen L.
Smith, Bertrand
Smith, Eli
Stanton, Henry G.
Starkey, James D.
Starks, Dana V.
Starks, Ronald
Steele, Gloria J.
Steele, Roger B.
Stephens, Alan G.
Stephens, Thomas
Stepney, Michael
Stevens, James P. Jr.
Steward, A.
Steward, James
Stewart, H. Jr.
Stewart, Jackie
Stokes, John
Stokes, Julius H.
Stoll, Carl B.
Strong, Larry Sr.
Strotter, Joseph H.
Strozier, D.
Sumerlin, Norman
Swain, Costell S.
Swanigan, Isiah
Swope, Thomas E.

Tarpley, H. Jr.
Tasker, D. R.
Tate, Johnny E
Taylor, L. E. Jr.

Spivey, Joe A.
Stanton, Charles

Taylor, William
Terry, Lawrence E.
Thomas, David
Thomas, Donald
Thomas, E. C. Jr.
Thomas, J. E
Thomas, James
Thomas, James
Thomas, Joseph S.
Thomas, Robert L.
Thomas, William
Thompson, Edward
Thompson, G.
Thompson, G. L.
Thompson, Jeffrey
Thompson, L. A.
Thompson, Rodney
Thorne, Robert C.
Threet, Michael A.
Tilford, Fred III
Toles, James R.
Toliver, James
Tolliver, Michael L.
Toney, Freddie L.
Tooles, Dennis L.
Toran, A. L. Jr.
Tribble, Charles
Tribble, Diann M.
Triche, Ronald S.

Taylor, Robert E.
Taylor, Theodore

Turner, Isaiah
Turner, Ralph I.
Turner, Thomas L.
Tyler, Calvin E.
Tyse, F. J.

Valentine, J. B. Jr.
Vinson, Robert A.

Wade, Thomas Jr.
Walker, Daisey M.
Walker, Richard M.
Walker, Willie J.
Wallace, Richard
Waller, Thomas S.
Walston, Carl L.
Walton, Eldge L.
Ward, Lonnie
Ward, Ray C.
Ware, Alfonso
Ware, Austin W.
Ware, Henry D.
Washington, C.
Washington, Earl
Washington, James
Washington, James
Washington, Len
Waters, E. L. Jr.
Watkins, D. W. Sr.

Tucker, William W.
Turnbough, Leon L.
Watson, Eugene
Watson, Henry Jr.
Webb, Kenneth M.
Webster, Stephen
West, James A.
West, Lepolia
Westbrook, J.
Wheat, Fred R.
Wheeler, V. A.
White, Charles M.
White, Joseph H.
White, Wayne E.
Wiley, James P.
Wiley, Raymond
Wilkerson, Fred
Williams, A. W.
Williams, Bobby
Williams, Charles
Williams, D. X.
Williams, E. L.
Williams, Eugene
Williams, F. E.
Williams, H. Jr.
Williams, I. Jr.
Williams, J. Jr.
Williams, Jimmie
Williams, John
Williams, L.
Willaims, Lee A.

Williams, L. J.

Watkins, Eugene
Watson, Carl
Williams, M. A.
Williams, Patrice
Williams, R. C.
Williams, Robert
Williams, Robert
Williams, Ronald
Williams, Teresa
Willis, Kirk J.
Wilson, Charles J.
Wilson, Harry Jr.
Wilson, Jimmie L.
Wilson, Sam H.
Wilson, W. Jr.
Wise, David
Witherspoon, D. C.
Womack, Emmit Jr.
Woods, Donald L.
Woods, Hedy
Woods, James A.
Woods, W. F.
Woodward, W. T.
Wortham, Homer E.
Wortham, T. E.
Wrightsell, L. C.
Wynn, Clifford

Yancy, A. Jr.
Yates, Troy L. Jr.
Young, Julius A.

For further research visit the Chicago History Museum, 1601 North Clark Street in Chicago, IL which has a comprehensive collection of the activities and history of the Afro American Police League from its inception.

For more information about the Positive Anti Crime Thrust (P.A.C.T.) visit www.positiveact.info

www.ingramcontent.com/pod-product-compliance
Lightning Source LLC
LaVergne TN
LVHW021720060526
838200LV00050B/2773